One Degree Beyond:
A Reiki Journey Into
Energy Medicine

ONE DEGREE BEYOND

A Reiki Journey Into Energy Medicine

LITTLE WHITE BUFFALO
PUBLISHING COTTAGE
SEATTLE, WA

JANEANNE NARRIN

LITTLE WHITE BUFFALO PUBLISHING COTTAGE
Creating Ladders to Pure Potential

For a free catalog or ordering information, write
Little White Buffalo Publishing Cottage, 12345 Lake City Way N.E., Suite 204
Seattle, Washington 98125
http://www.onedegreebeyond.com

or fax
425/673-9325

This book is manufactured in the United States of America.
Cover art by Nichole Parsons
Book design by Houghton-Blessing

Published by Little White Buffalo Publishing Cottage
12345 Lake City Way N.E., Suite 204
Seattle, Washington 98125

Narrin, Janeanne.
1. new consciousness 2. personal growth
3. alternative medicine

ISBN 0-9658545-5-8

10 9 8 7 6 5 4 3 2 1

**THIS BOOK IS PRINTED ON
RECYCLED PAPER**

Because...
"Significant consensus has emerged concerning the threats facing the planet's biological diversity and biological health. Scientists, activist and government officials increasingly are united in their conviction that humankind's unrestrained industrial activities in general, and the widespread and accelerating decline of forests in particular, are degrading the biosphere. Less progress has been made in communicating to the general public the consequences of the rapid impoverishment of biological systems we are now experiencing..."

Glen Barry, Director,
Ecological Enterprises, http://www.forests.org

"Just trust life:
Life will bring you high,
If only you are careful in selecting
In the maze of events,
Those influences or those paths
Which can bring you each time
A little more upward.

Life has to be discovered
And built step by step
A great charm..."

Pierre Teilhard de Chardin

Contents

Foreword by Paula Horan, Ph.D.
Acknowledgments
Author's Note
Introduction

PART ONE: EXPLORATION

Chapter 1: Relax, Open, Celebrate

Chapter 2: Fortuitous Detours... Change and Innovation

Chapter 3: About Reiki

Chapter 4: Usui: A Reiki Journey Into Energy Medicine

Chapter 5: One Degree Beyond

An Interlude: The Reiki Break

PART TWO: APPLICATION

Chapter 6: Keys to an Unfolding Process

Chapter 7: The Reiki Methodology
A Participatory Model

Chapter 8: Participatory Themes and the Reiki Session

Chapter 9: Relax, Open, Celebrate! A 21-Day Program for Reiki and Relaxation

APPENDICES

Appendix A: Making Contact

Appendix B: Complementary Systems

Appendix C: Resources

Appendix D: A Quiz

FOREWORD
By Paula Horan, Ph.D.

Janeanne Narrin's long career in personnel psychology has provided her with extensive insight into the cause and possible solutions to negative (or "bad" stress) in the present working world. With broad experience as a corporate headhunter, she is skilled in the ways of the world. She is also a gifted painter and poet with a corresponding point of view. Due to her varied life experience, Janeanne has encountered both the intense stress of the corporate world and the silent, healing, meditative state of the artist. The pages that follow are a joy to experience as she draws you in with her incredible ability to "talk story" and wax poetic in her own unique style. She has the gift of being able to address the high-powered, left-brained, Type-A personality, opening him or her to the possibilities of the peaceful state of silent "beingness" which Reiki evokes. This is in contrast to the state most people experience (whether left- or right-brained), which is limited to the "Doer" or ego-centered consciousness from which most of the world is still suffering and trying desperately (albeit unconsciously) to move beyond.

Janeanne opens a door for the reader to go deeper into the process of Reiki than in most other books. Having practiced Reiki for several years before moving into her mastership, she is well grounded in her perception of Universal Reiki and fully demonstrates her ability to convey its essence. Indeed, her gift as a healer and teacher enable her to "De-mystify" Reiki without taking the mystery out of it!

Janeanne points the way to the direct experience of Reiki clearly, as she helps the reader to find that Reiki, *as pure heart energy*, is beyond mind and cannot be understood. Reiki can be perceived through the "vision" of the heart; and heart knowledge is perceived through the transference and open reception of love. Reiki, as Universal

"... pure heart energy is beyond mind..."
Paula Horan

Life-force Energy, *is* the very energy of Heart. When used consciously, it can put us in touch with deeper understandings. Without words, it can allow us to relax and to enjoy the unlimited potential that we are.

For the uninitiated, Reiki has become a global phenomenon. Insurance companies are even considering giving remuneration for Reiki treatments due to their purported healing benefits. Janeanne Narrin's special emphasis on Reiki's results when used to counter *stress* may further promote its popularity, but more than this, it offers immediate accessibility to a system that presents an alternative for preventative *self* care.

Paula Horan, Ph.D.
author of *Empowerment Through Reiki*
and *Abundance Through Reiki*

ACKNOWLEDGMENTS

No book is the work of a single individual, and I wish to acknowledge and to thank the many teachers, past and present, who have contributed so much to my own understanding of the process of self-discovery and empowerment.

Special appreciation to the following people whose wise words and insights are included in this book: Pat and Bob Green, Tonie and C.B., David and Bonnyrae, Maliki, Ann, Bruce, Rob and Helen, Nancy, Joan, Tracy and Tom, Christi, Cherie, Jerry, Andrea, Norman and Lynn, Heidemarie, Nicole and Randy, Therese, Charlie and Cleo, Wendi, Fred, Mary and Carolyn, Fabian, Tom and Faye, Cathy and Steve, Garreth, Jim and Michelle, Hazel, Russ, Regina, and David.

Bless you, Joan Marie, and Norm, wherever you are.

To my mentors in the corporate world, Judy Bankey, Louise DePutron, John Goldsworthy, John Hale, Jim Hanje, Andy Hasley, John and Nancy Kufchock, Sam Mancuso, Mike Mikolay, Tom Moylan, Terry Murphy, Tony Raubolt, Steve Sicotte-Kelly, Bernie Wesol, three grateful bows.

Thanks to Reiki Master, Paula Horan, Ph.D., whose energy and frankness delight her friends, Reiki Masters Wanja Twan, Rick Bockner, Earlene Gleisner, Mari Hall, Norma Jean Young, Becky Farrar-Koch and Jo Angelina for their support, and to Phyllis Lei Furumoto for just *being* who you are. To my students, who have shared their wisdom with me, thanks for your encouragement.

Applause to those who took time to read and reread the manuscript, and offer editorial comment – to Matthias, editorial wizard, Diann, Mike, Jo, David, Karen and Jeremy, John, and to my best critic and friend, Steve. Special thanks to Lauren Houghton, whose valor through the fire is amazing, and to Ann Elniff, and Faye Kendall whose dedication and word processing skills were invaluable.

To Lara Lavi, The Poet Schrecengost, Lee Henderson and Wind-in-the-Feather, whose poetry speaks to me, thank you.

To King James the Cat, who often sat upon the manuscript, imbuing it with the happy energy of resonant Maine Coon purrs, and to dear Goldendog, Maggie, there from the start, my warmest appreciation.

Finally, special thanks to my father, Edward Aloysius O'Donnell, for his steadfast interest in this book, and to my son, John Thomas Narrin, for his way of saying just the right thing at just the right time.

$\mathcal{A}$UTHOR'S NOTE

Throughout this book, stories illustrate various aspects of Reiki energy. A person described in a story may actually be a composite of several characters. Many vignettes include exchanges drawn verbatim from tapes, or notes taken during Reiki sessions or workshops. Some have been edited for clarification, but the quotations represent exactly what was said.

Although this book addresses viable self-healing methods, it is not intended to offer recommendations or advice for the treatment of specific physical disease. Please, consult your qualified health practitioner or physician before entering any form of therapy.

INTRODUCTION

Every life has at its core a dream that quietly and unobtrusively asks to be fulfilled. Each of us dreams such a dream. It is an important part of the original blessing of being in this world. *Purpose* is another word for this dream. If you wish to realize your purpose in life you best start by relaxing. Relaxation allows for an open, unbounded, creative space. In this openness you can celebrate, that is, apply yourself, exercise your talents within the healthy boundaries of your chosen field or profession, get what you want, and not give it away, but share it wisely. Relaxing, opening and celebrating – three simple steps to individual well-being.

Woven into the formula for individual well-being is a need for supporting the global community bringing our human endeavors into alignment with a *partnership* model of reality. This means that everybody wins. Although based on self-interest, everyone's actions contribute to the highest good of all concerned. In their prayers our Native American brothers and sisters refer to this extended sense of community as "all of our relations". All of our relations of our global community comprise our fellow humans, the animals, plants, minerals: the rocks, mountains and seas, the deserts, swamps and wetlands, the great plains and wild forests.

How can we effectively support them? We could introduce ever more new and tighter legislation – adopt stringent rules and regulations. We have seen how this plan works. And about its effectiveness there can be no illusions. Laws created by man are manipulative and subject to manipulation. Rules can be bent and regulations have loopholes. Furthermore, rules and regulations imply that we are ignorant of universal or natural law. By their very existence they infer that we do not inherently know, feel or sense what is right, but rather, because of our ignorance, must submit to some outside authority. Poised between ourselves and the world, laws, rules and regulations may even widen the gulf of separation between ourselves and nature.

The benefit of "all of our relations" really cannot be decreed from the outside. Founded on interconnectedness, it unfolds through understanding, and through assimilating and growing into universal law. It amounts to a deep healing partnership process—an empathic resonance, between nature and humankind.

If we wish to support and restructure our global community in genuinely new and liberating ways, we cannot do so just by the decree of manmade law. Instead, we have to start closer to home, with ourselves, our personal integrity, our own energy. In other words, we have to become ourselves, whole and healthy individuals. We have to think for ourselves, wean ourselves away from undue outside influence, take good care of ourselves emotionally and physically, and follow our purpose in life – and we have to be open and intuitively grasp the particular strands of universal law that apply in a given situation.

In the energetic model of reality there is no separation. Focusing upon our own wholehearted well-being, letting it flow through our lives and out to others, will eventually help manifest a wholesome and healthy global community. There are many different tools for such transformation. Reiki is one of them.

One Degree Beyond presents Reiki, the practice of the ancient art of healing, in the wider framework of energy medicine and boldly proposes that we are dual citizens of the energetic and physical realms. Not only do we have bodies and minds, but we also partake in and embody the very energies that create the universe – and this in our perception – moment by moment anew. This energy is our most precious resource and can be directly accessed.

Years ago, the "100th monkey" theory was widely popular and often quoted. It went like this: if, one by one, a hundred monkeys on a distant island learn how to use sticks for picking bananas the knowledge of picking bananas with sticks all of a sudden becomes an integral part of monkey consciousness. All monkeys everywhere all around the world will then be privy to this knowledge and be able to use sticks to that end.

The principle of a vanguard few preparing a shift in consciousness applies to humankind as well and has inspired many changes in past history. Understanding this, we do not see Reiki merely as a solace for people in need, and definitely not as a sophisticated and blissfully esoteric pacifier for the ones who choose to endlessly wallow in their woundedness. We rather know it to be an energy of powerful positive change that in the hands of certain agents of change can contribute to a desperately needed shift in consciousness for our global community. Anyone can be such an agent of change, but the more dedicated you are to what you are doing the more impact you will have as an agent of change.

Generally, Reiki is described as a gentle hands-on technique of energy exchange rediscovered a little over a century ago in Meji-era Japan by Dr. Mikao Usui and transmitted to the present day through an unbroken line of successors and practitioners. Quite a few books have been published on the subject, but here we are exploring the process of Reiki from the vantage of cutting-edge science.

If the practice of Reiki is to become the truly transformative experience that it can be, one would have to avoid the trap of reinterpreting this experience along the lines of outmoded beliefs and models of thinking which rely on a subject/object polarity. This totally obscures the field within which the dance of subject and object unfolds in the first place. By blotting out the field, we deprive ourselves of its nourishing qualities. The force, then, cannot be with us.

To counteract our proclivity for heroically remaining stuck in the same old rut of reductionist distortions *One Degree Beyond* (as in one degree beyond the apparent choices of outmoded thinking) elucidates the very practical and applicable relationship between Reiki and modern scientific thinking and uses the tools of self-inquiry to open new doors of perception.

Part One

Exploration

Relax, Open, Celebrate...

Imagine.

Imagine walking barefoot.
Imagine walking barefoot on a
path of fragrant bark...
Feeling the summer sun on your
head, and the warmth on your
feet...
Reaching down with your hands...
Extending, to touch that bark...
Holding shape, form, texture...
And knowing, in a way you've
never known before.

Imagine, as you walk on,
And, as the path opens out into
yellow sunlight,
Giving way under foot to sweet,
green grass,
That you pause to look about.

There, within sight, lies a grove
Whose tender blossoms grace this
day, and
A golden hammock
Suspended 'neath the trees
Sways
To beckon you.

Oh, how your very Being vibrates
with this pulsing place
And, now, from the hammock
Suspended 'neath those trees
Suspended in Space,
Suspended in Time,
You own the Moment...
Feel whole,
At peace,

Imagine.

Wind-in-the-Feather

---

*"The voyage of discovery lies not in finding new landscapes,
but in having new eyes."*

Marcel Proust

A Place to Relax

In the Stone Age while our hairy ancestors were timidly peering from caves, fleeing ravenous foes, wrestling with gods of wind and rain, they were also writing the first chapter of the Book of Stress. Anxiety is at least as old as we are, however, our "harried" contemporaries, in a modern-day version of the above, have added a few exotic twists to manifest stress: we've intensified it. Our fast-paced society, with its technological advances and wide-ranging lifestyles even promotes pressure, and whether this be of global or lesser magnitude, it seems relentless.

Without a method for being mindful of the opportunities that exist within the maelstrom, we may remain unable to really celebrate life. In order to seize the moment while maintaining our equilibrium in the dance of our days, we would be wise to create a personal sanctuary. Not everyone has a real place—a beach house, a remote campsite, a hilltop retreat; but everyone needs, and indeed can have a nonphysical destination, a special timeless space to call upon…such is Reiki (Ray-kee).

This tool for relaxation opens new doors of perception to demonstrate both a wonderful ocean of energy and a system for working *with* that energy. The effect is a spacious and exhilarating sense – or state of being. You might describe this as feeling as if you were suspended in a hammock of pure potential.

No caves for us! When life's out of joint, we can consider the possibilities, and Reiki.

There are two ways to know Reiki and its possibilities. The first way, experiencing it, is the most important, and you may already know Reiki in that manner. You could even become aware of it before you finish this page. However, it is not something that you can learn from this book. You see, most people who discover Reiki do not start with a book. They start with an experience.

The practical meaning of Reiki (as used when it refers to the mindful practice) is a method for touching which generates a difference. The person engaging in the practice knows that something new, and very welcomed, has happened. After you have that experience, even simple things such as reading a book are seen through different eyes. You seem to already know and understand the most important aspects because of that direct experience which addresses and answers the skeptic in all of us.

The second way to know Reiki lies in how to evoke the experience; the one that makes you certain that something real, and refreshing has happened. You do not have to believe anything in particular to have this learning. You could be like the electrician who does not believe in electrons, but who can wire a building perfectly. Someone who knows how to "plug in" to Reiki can teach you how.

Just remember: Reiki does not commence with a lot of theory that tells you that if you meditate and exercise for years you will attain a state that you can only imagine now. It starts with the experience. Something important happens with Reiki. It happened for me when I was not expecting anything, and it can also happen for you.

"In all activities of life, from trivial to important, the secret of efficiency lies in the ability to combine two seemingly incompatible states... a state of maximum activity, and a state of maximum relaxation."

Aldous Huxley

Stress as Opportunity

Many people come to appreciate the rewards of relaxing only after having immersed themselves in prolonged periods of "battling the enemy."

In our present day highly charged and competitive society, where world markets rely on high-tech communications and speed is the byword, power players press the limits of endurance on many levels. One need not be a corporate executive climbing the "ladder of success" to enter the fray. Frazzled folks come in home-brewed varieties, too—or ask an inner-city teacher about his "beat." Things seem to be pretty intense these days. What better environment for advancing the practice of relaxation!

Most people view stress as either good or bad. What would happen if we saw it as opportunity? What if by examining the raw stuff of "bad" stress, by really getting down to the basics, by making a realistic assessment of our stressors, we came to know life as a celebration?

Looking closely at "bad" stress seems a good place to start.

"One of the most damaging consequences of looking to the world to satisfy our inner needs is a competitive mode of consciousness... It promotes blinkered thinking and shortsightedness.."

Peter Russell
The White Hole in Time

Recent USA Polls:

- Percentage of people frustrated by the deterioration of the environment: 80.
- Percentage of people dissatisfied with their lives: 74.
- Percentage of people whose doctor visits are stress related: over 70.
- Percentage of high school students suffering from stress:

Dr. Michael Cohen
Re-Connecting with Nature

Looking at "Bad" Stress

*M*ost cavefolk today view "good" stress as a motivator, and equate "bad" stress with losing their sense of internal equilibrium. Then, tension may seem overwhelming. An alarm jangles causing us to look just as wild eyed as our Stone Age ancestors.

This is a natural response.

Usually, the first place we notice imbalance is in our bodies. Here, "bad" stress can prompt abnormal amounts of hormones to flow from the adrenal glands. This shrinks the thymus, which, in turn taxes the whole immune system, setting up a chain reaction. The body becomes susceptible to any number of maladies.

But before this happens, your body will tell you. All you have to do is pay attention and get the message… as in the chart on the following page..

How the Body Communicates
Stress

When the body signals distress in any or all of the following ways, it can be an opportunity to reevaluate priorities, and redirect our energies. Check applicable boxes below.

Symptom:	Level of Stress You Experience:		
	Light	Moderate	Extreme
Alarm Reactions	❏	❏	❏
Aggression	❏	❏	❏
Anger	❏	❏	❏
Angst	❏	❏	❏
Anxiety	❏	❏	❏
Apathy	❏	❏	❏
Asthma	❏	❏	❏
Back Pain	❏	❏	❏
Blue Moods	❏	❏	❏
Body "Aches"	❏	❏	❏
Boredom	❏	❏	❏
Cancer	❏	❏	❏
Chronic Muscle Strain	❏	❏	❏
Cold Sweats	❏	❏	❏
Confusion	❏	❏	❏
Tension	❏	❏	❏
Depression	❏	❏	❏
Digestion problems	❏	❏	❏
Dizziness	❏	❏	❏
Dry Mouth	❏	❏	❏
Eating Disorders	❏	❏	❏
Excessive Drinking	❏	❏	❏
Fatigue	❏	❏	❏
Grumpy Moods	❏	❏	❏
Headache	❏	❏	❏

	Light	Moderate	Extreme
Heart Arrhythmia	☐	☐	☐
Heart Attack	☐	☐	☐
High Blood Pressure	☐	☐	☐
Hives	☐	☐	☐
Insomnia	☐	☐	☐
Irritability	☐	☐	☐
Loss of Sexual Interest	☐	☐	☐
Melancholy Moods	☐	☐	☐
Overspending, Overeating	☐	☐	☐
Poor Impulse Control	☐	☐	☐
Rashes	☐	☐	☐
Restlessness	☐	☐	☐
Skepticism	☐	☐	☐
Skin Disorders	☐	☐	☐
Sleep Disturbance	☐	☐	☐
Sleeplessness	☐	☐	☐
Temper "Tantrums"	☐	☐	☐
Tightness in Chest	☐	☐	☐
Ulcers	☐	☐	☐
Worrisome Thoughts	☐	☐	☐

How the Body Communicates Stress
Check-In

Physical:

> *Stress manifests itself in various ways. Check-in with yourself in the following areas. Note signs, symptoms and how tension is expressing itself.*

Mental:

Emotional:

Relationships:

Inner-Spirit:

> *"People who involve themselves in nature reconnecting activities reduce their stress and disorders."*
>
> *Dr. Michael Cohen*

What is the message for you?

Try this:

Find a hilltop campsite far from city lights and sounds. Pack a picnic and blankets and settle in there watching the earth spin away from the sun ("sunset") and the stars as they appear in the sky. Lie on your side and look OUT (not up) at the stars. Now visualize yourself on the curved surface of the Earth — halfway down (not on "top") again looking OUT. You are <u>part</u> of the planet, held in place by gravity. Next, arrive at a mental picture of yourself on the "bottom" of the globe, looking DOWN at the stars. You are an integral part of this cosmos. What can you learn from this?

*   **Adaptation of an experiment in "rapid reorganization of phenomenon" ...*

*   Brian Swimme, Ph.D*
<u>*The Hidden Heart of the Cosmos*</u>

A System for Going Within

*A*nticipation and defense, whether communicated as physical, emotional or mental messages, translate into *tension*. This indicator of mind-body interaction though alarming, can be positive, for when the interaction goes awry, an opportunity also arises for us to be more attentive to ourselves and to others. We can then reevaluate and redirect our lives while gaining fresh perspectives. All that is needed is a key for unlocking the door to that potential... and that key is the practice of Reiki.

The practice of Reiki reveals that a universal capacity to heal and to celebrate life is contained within our very nature, where an extraordinary power to put events in our lives in context leads to the understanding of our participation in an unfolding universe.

If we listen to what our bodies communicate to us, we can slip through the barriers of illusion, using "bad" stress as a springboard to lift us into a higher, broader vision of our reality. Indeed, we may even discover our unique place in a universe new science describes as one whole, interacting, resonating mass of pulsating energy.

fresh perspectives

There is a "rapid reorganization of phenomena" when one comes to this realization, and it relates directly to celebrating life!

"... the opportunity of our time is to integrate science's understanding of the universe with more ancient intuitions concerning the meaning and destiny of the human. The promise of this work is that through such an enterprise, the human species as a whole will begin to embrace a common meaning and a coherent program of action..."

Brian Swimme, Ph.D.
The Hidden Heart of the Cosmos

"What is demanded of us now is to change attitudes that are so deeply bound into our basic cultural patterns that they seem to us as an imperative of the very nature of our being, a dictate of our genetic coding as a species. In clinical language, we are in a deep cultural pathology. We can no longer trust our cultural guidance in any comprehensive manner. In this situation we must return to our genetic structure and rethink who we are, where we fit into the community of existence, and what our proper role might be within this community."

Thomas Berry, Ph.D.
Ethics and Ecology,
A paper delivered at Harvard University, 1996

An Emerging Understanding

*7*he universe is one whole, interacting, interconnected, interrelated, organic energy system in which what affects the one effects the whole in the unfolding dance of life.

This emerging understanding, and its impact upon us, is slowly coming into the popular mind. To grasp its significance requires considerable diligence and perceptual reorientation on our part. Each of us would be wise to reflect upon the implications.

The practice of Reiki supports such a contemplative enterprise, but before expanding on this, let's take a look at a contextual framework:

Our societal structure has been based on a mechanistic model. Now we are coming to see that a different reality exists beyond and alongside this familiar one. We are coming to understand that we are not separate from one another (no matter how it appears that way)— not separate from the Natural World.

If we integrate this relatively new understanding into our everyday lives, if we find a way to see with our inner-vision, listen with our inner-hearing, feel with our inner-heart, it becomes possible to supersede outmoded Newtonian definitions to manifest a transformative shift in consciousness.

This cannot come too soon, since many indicators direct us to observe the swing of the pendulum which, throughout history has warned us of painful extremes. But we have also discovered that Pain is the great dissolver of Illusion. It is the impetus for change and balance. Because of Pain, we can awake to hear the message... to listen to what is happening, and to let this sink into our consciousness... which in turn allows us to resonate with the ground of all Being. As we awaken, we realize that our challenge is to be open to forces which would keep us in tune with our ultimate concerns.

You know, we tend to be in our own little niches... work, commutes, errands, family matters... plodding the old treadmill, and remaining narrowly focused. Thus, we need to remember to pay attention, to recognize where we are and where we need to be, so that as individuals and as a global community we can rise to the level of our true potential as Creatures of Limitlessness. One degree beyond paying attention, is resonating with *Universal Life-force Energy* and Balance.

To be so attuned means that we have to stop doing things unnatural... stop blocking out openness to Life. From this perspective, we may convey a brave new vision.

A Warning to Humanity

"Human beings and the Natural World are set on a collision course. If not checked, many of our current practices put at serious risk the future we wish for Human Society, and the Plant and Animal Kingdoms – and may so alter the living world that it will be unable to sustain life in the manner that we know..."

Union of Concerned Scientists

Only the Brave

A more refined view of our understanding of reality is at hand, but the stressful context in which it is packaged may be so all-encompassing, that we avoid assimilating this new imperative. A traditional, dualistic, "parts" mentality is driven by fear. Only the brave can move beyond accustomed points of reference. Only the brave ask serious and probing questions about our physical and energetic nature. Only the brave open the door through contemplation, to step into a new way of seeing and celebrating life.

Hard Questions

1. What is the larger significance of the human enterprise in an unfolding universe?

2. How can we replace outmoded ways of seeing the world and bridge the vast expanses between the multidimensional realms of body, mind and inner spirit, technology and spirituality?

3. What is our responsibility and our place in the living global community?

4. What wisdom is needed to restore balance within our microcosmic and macrocosmic realities?

5. Has anyone seen the ladder to <u>Beyond</u>?

Ladders and Solutions

"In order to solve a problem, you must first understand the problem and then what you can do to solve it."

In order to solve a problem, you must first understand the problem and then what you can do to solve it. Often, if we are willing to just start where we are, a way opens up for us. It may well be that our communal best interest hinges on allotting the timespace to relax into a new understanding of the realities of our existence. These discoveries are just one degree beyond the apparent. They are, however, accessible through the practice of Reiki—and here may begin a journey into powerful energy medicine. I took such a journey not that many years ago. A series of fortuitous detours taught me to follow the signposts. It happened for me when I was not expecting anything. And it can also happen for you.

Fortuitous Detours...
Change and Innovation

2

Synchronicity

Today,
not out of planning,
striving
longing
wisdom, or celebrity,
but merely by chance
as I sat in all solemnity
regarding my breath as it fell and
rose,

Today,
a butterfly brushed my nose
and I,
regarding its faerie wings
beheld, at last,
the Land of Kings!

Wind-in-the-Feather

"The ground of the universe is an empty fullness, a fecund nothingness...the base of the universe seethes with creativity... 'space- time- foam'"

Brian Swimme, Ph.D.
The Hidden Heart of the Cosmos

Signposts and Directions

Sometimes, when one is searching for answers and least expects it, one's life takes a fantastic turn, as synchronicity plays tricks on stale perceptions, and timing or luck reveals change and innovation. There must have been the delightful potential for "being in the right place at the right time" operating, when I encountered a series of fortuitous detours not all that many years ago, and inadvertently awoke to a new vision just one degree beyond the apparent.

I was taking an inspiration break one winter, one of the perks self-employment affords me, to motor west with my golden retriever, Maggie. The 4-wheeler was packed for adventure and we headed out in high anticipation of what a long, back-road trip might reveal.

As a management consultant specializing in career and personnel issues, I had plenty on my mind. Business friends I met every day were dropping by the wayside from chronic fatigue, ulcers, burnout, even heart attacks. I had been gathering statistics for a corporate study, but just recording the facts seemed so futile. I wanted to *do* something about the situation. So while for Maggie this trip meant exotic smells, strange territories, and excellent food in doggie

"The subtle Way of the universe gave birth to a world of peace and order.

It responds to the order and harmony of all beings and things.

Without needing to talk with them.
Without your summoning it, it comes to you.
Without scheming, its plan is perfect.
Vast is the subtle energy network of the universe.
Sparsely meshed it is, yet nothing can slip through it."

Lao Tzu

bags, my agenda included: 1) unscheduled serious thinking; 2) openness to opportunity; and, 3) the willingness to follow the signposts as they pointed out new directions.

We set out from Boston in a snow squall and for the first few days crept further and further south hoping to avoid icy road conditions. No sooner would I decide to take a route than sleet would change the plan until we were headed due south. A sense of actually being urged along by some force beyond the control of mere mortals overtook me. "Of course, one does not really *expect* to exert control over Mother Nature," I reasoned, between wiper slaps. Nonetheless, as the dog and I detoured to an even *more* southerly path now headed straight for Santa Fe, New Mexico… trying to outrun the freezing cold… only to run into another blizzard… that absolutely forbade further travel… I could not escape a sense of destiny. There was nothing to do but trust the "gods of the changing seasons."

Thus began a charmed voyage…into a realm beyond any I had known before.

Santa Fe: Paying Attention

In a steady snowfall, "Good Ole' Gold" and I safely slid into Santa Fe, but we could go no farther. Deciding to capitalize on this unexpected twist of fate, we found lodging, then set out on foot to absorb the unique ambiance of the town, as well as to locate the gallery where the work of Amado Peña is displayed. Peña captures the spirit of high desert native peoples. He softens the boundaries of time, allowing us to recognize our kinship in a timeless realm – a very balancing notion.

I began thinking how a "certain" finely crafted silver, coral and turquoise ring, my lucky piece - had that quality, too… and smiled to myself as I recalled how it had found its way to me.

Ten years ago, that lucky ring had belonged to an itinerant crew member of the *Western Ice Capades* and had been the centerpiece of her liquid savings account; handy for trade or barter. It, and other Old Pawn items, rolled snuggly in a jewelers bag, had traversed the country. She had acquired it in a dramatic way.

As she told it, she'd been sitting at the counter in a truck stop near Tucumcari - just "minding her own business" - having a piece of lemon meringue pie, listening to old honky-tonk tunes around midnight, when the ring literally had slipped off the gesturing hand of a smooth-shaven cowboy who was seated next to her. She had already studied his Stetson hat and shiny boots, so when the ring dropped with a thud next to her cup of coffee, she took the opportunity to raise her eyebrows, and smile, openly at him. Now, seeing her surprised look, that smooth dude from the prairies "fessed up" as to how he'd won the ring from a pueblo kid in a poker game "back down the road a-piece, and sorta reckoned it shouldn't even be his… cuz, it once belonged to a medicine man," or at least that's what the kid had told him when he handed it over… "Kinda spooks me," he admitted. She thought to herself how nicely it would fit in her little "savings account" jewelers bag. He was saying that it sure was too big for him… and he didn't mind if she "wanted to take it off his hands, since the ring seemed to prefer her, anyway…" and he winked at her. She returned the favor and the conversation, and by the end of the evening the ring was hers –"for a fair price". I didn't dare ask what that was, although the tone of her voice implied that yet another story lingered there. I found out only that she was pleased that someone else's folly was her good fortune. Not long after that, she returned home to await the birth of her "miracle baby."

I happened upon her while she was unable to work and desperate for funds. The moment she unfurled her Old Pawn collection, I was struck by that same ring. I had the most definite sense that it liked me. "That's silly!", I thought, as I negotiated a "fair price." It was almost as if it sprouted little feathery wings and transported itself right into my palm. And it wasn't long until I noticed its unique charms…

Until that day in Santa Fe, I had never tried to justify my attachment to this remarkable ring, nor the uncanny feeling that its story was still unfolding, but now, as we threaded our way through the freezing slush on the streets of this historic town, I found myself wondering if it had once come from a pueblo nearby…

As Maggie and I sloshed down Palace Avenue, towards the oldest public building in the United States I remarked how history impresses itself in Santa Fe. Traditional methods, which had supplied artifacts of old, flourish, and ancient arts are still practiced by skilled artisans. Some present-day objects are little changed in form and construct from those of a thousand years ago. I began to notice how aptly the ring reflected these things… but wait, here was Peña's place! I halted, transfixed. A canvas, almost the width of a barn door and as tall, greeted me as I entered. Not only was it enormous, but unlike the more subdued pallets of his earlier canvases, this work arrested my attention with its bold strokes and slashes of red. Musing about the ring ceased.

But the Muse would not be denied.

The very next day while icy rains continued to delay travel, the ring once more insisted on inching into my thoughts, when I found myself fascinated with certain small bear carvings of the Zuni tribe. Time and again, my fingers traced the grooves and smooth surfaces of these beautifully executed figures, until I discerned, at last, their appeal to me. That same timeless spirit enveloped these small stone forms too! Most evocative of all were the diminutive pieces of a particular master carver, these came home with me. Something here spoke to my heart as did the whispering ring. Was it just in the execution, I wondered?...

*"The soul should always stand ajar, ready to welcome
the ecstatic experience."*

Emily Dickinson

A Teacher

"...when the student is ready..."

*A*s chance would have it, a former teacher from Zuni, now the owner of a gallery I visited in Santa Fe, provided the next clue to the ring's evolving tale. That afternoon found me at her gallery, where we talked at length about her experiences with the Zuni people, their culture and beliefs... including how Zuni fetishes represented archetypal wisdom. After some time, she disclosed that she actually knew the man who had carved those I had chosen. "He's a blind medicine man whose hands have their own eyes," she reported. "He lives on the Zuni Reserve." As she spoke on, my thoughts wandered to that man, and I began trying to visualize in my own mind's eye just how he would carve the intricate bear forms... began wondering how he lived... what his life was like... what it would be like to stay always in one place... how he saw things with an inner-sight... and how he could bring such energy into tiny carvings... with hands with their own eyes. Then, suddenly, returning to the moment, and curious to see if the teacher, too, saw the design similarities, I retrieved the ring and bear fetishes from my bag and placed them side-by-side on her ample wooden counter.

"Do you think these are all Zuni pieces?" I inquired. I was at once gratified when she nodded recognition (all *were* Zuni), and perplexed, as she drew in a sharp breath. She seemed so startled by the ring that I proceeded to tell her what I knew of the ring's story. "There's much more to it," she ventured, then urged me to travel to the Zuni Reserve. Something in me said, "Onward!" and when I agreed to go, she headed into her office humming mysteriously. Reappearing after a short time with two sealed envelopes in hand, she seemed almost breathless. Now with a glowing smile and a hug, she sent me on my way, her eyes twinkling with untold delight.

I had made myself a promise to be "open to ladders of opportunity" and "willing to follow signposts" along the way. Mother Nature had made the travel arrangements and now Zuni called to me. As I turned out the light that evening, the words of the Teacher played over and over in my mind - "There's more to it… There's more to it…" and soon a medicine man of inner sight smiled to himself and sang in my dreams… as a spider spun a golden web.

Early the next day, bearing messages to her friend, and to the one who had carved my bear fetishes, the golden-one-with-wagging-tail and I, set out for Zuni. It was the first sunny day that week. The roads were clear.

In the gentle morning hours, the lands surrounding Santa Fe always appear full of melody and movement. Undulating hills breathe shadows. The landscape resounds with a beat of its own, and the wind murmurs tones known only in the high desert. Aromas of piñon pine, and sage, with which the air is ever pungent, complement a scene of uncluttered vegetation. This is all perfectly punctuated with an infinite variety of striking landforms. These not duplicated in any other part of the world, greet the ascending sun, jutting their points into azure skies, as if they wish to release the deepest hues of blue to spread across the country with dazzling intensity. On this morning however, through all this beauty, and all this energy, there emerged in me a sense of cosmic belonging and profound gratitude.

Maggie, with ears and nose twitching, perched expectantly on the passenger seat of the trusty 4-wheeler. She was excited. We were both excited. "Hands have their own eyes," I told her, and speculated about what lay before us in Zuni.

"When we are unhurried and wise we perceive that only great and worthy things have any permanent and absolute existence - that petty fears, and petty pleasures are but the shadow of reality."

Henry David Thoreau

Zuni: Emptying

We wound our way past the Rio Grande, toward the southwest sector of New Mexico and the Zuni Reserve. Hours later, the road opened to a small town of weathered, one-story buildings lining the main street. Even though I felt as though I, as an individual, had been encouraged to come here, I also wondered whether we were but intruders in these lands, that have been home for the Anasazi Nation and its children for thousands of years.

Spotting the address, I found a parking space and emerged from my vehicle messages and heart in hand. Maggie padded along beside me, attentively. She planted herself, resolutely, by the doorway of the artists' co-op, which was my destination. Breathing deeply, I crossed the threshold; Maggie's eyes followed me.

All activity within the work room ceased, as I entered—alone. Ten pairs of Zuni eyes regarded me closely and, within that suspenseful instant, I could also picture the time when Coronado had led an expeditionary force in gilded armor (with metal helmets sporting plumes) against the unarmed, peace-loving Zuni farming communities. It saddened me to think how exploitation has characterized Zuni history, (and the history of humankind) and has extended into our own times with invaders of another kind. These plundered sacred ruins, leaving tourists slinging videocams (bent on aggressive sight-seeing) a legacy of scandal with the indigenous peoples. There was tension in the air.

"I was hoping to speak with the master carver," I began, tentatively. "I have messages from the Teacher in Santa Fe." A senior member of the group approached me. I handed her the first note. She read it, folded it, and put it in the pocket of her business suit, without uttering a word. Then excusing herself politely, she returned to the others (all women in skirts or jeans). There ensued animated conversation, gasps, and glances in my direction as she relayed information and I felt increasingly self-conscious. I could feel my pale skin turning various shades of red as those dark eyes looked at me once more. Then in a fluid movement, she turned and spoke with authority. "He is not here. But, you are welcome. Please come in," she said pleasantly. "Apparently, our friend in Santa Fe views you as a sister of the Bear Clan."

I smiled in relief and nodded, hoping she didn't notice my odd skin tone, naive as to what she meant by "sister of the Bear Clan," but appreciative of the acceptance. Though trembling, I managed to hand over the other note (written to the carver) as she guided me across the roughly-finished floor to what looked like a onetime grocery display case containing a sizable array of his creations.

Now the woman before me took on the same glow as the teacher in Santa Fe... as she deftly removed an elegant rock-red fetish from the top shelf. Every detail was hand-perfected, each curve rounding into the next. Even the turn of the head was alert. How I longed to know how hands could have eyes of their own. "The Old Carver would want you to have this bloodstone bear," she announced, "he finished it last night and brought it with him when he came in with his family earlier today." As I started to decline, she placed her hand on mine and continued...

"You know, many years ago a "certain ring"... finely-crafted, silver, coral and turquoise... handed down from a medicine elder... was gambled away in a poker game to a cowboy in a Stetson hat... is it true that you know this story?"

"Good Heavens!!" I exclaimed, stunned by the question.

A dizzying realization was sweeping over me, as my recently red skin paled to a bloodless white. My heart and mind struggled to assimilate the meaning of that moment... of coincidence and fate...of trust and letting go... of finding needles in haystacks... and lucky charms who sprout feathery wings.

I had carried that clever ring with me every day for years. It had accompanied me as I won consulting contracts with IBM, Hewlett Packard, and Sun Microsystems; indeed, whenever I made senior-level presentations. It always jangled in my bag reminding me of a universe of abundant blessings; an ungainly lucky token. More than just a charm, it had come to be a symbol of personal integrity to me. As such, it was also a reminder of an aspect of spiritual value.

If this ring had a "special energy," it also had a fairy tale story; for, after all these years (and a few detours) *it had found its way back to the place where it belonged* !

As I stood, speechless, from a place deep within me, I knew that the time had come for me to release it. Could I do it? Could I detach from my fondness for it, and the feeling of security it represented, to celebrate its enchanting "homing" powers?

As the Zuni woman's warm hand placed the now warm bloodstone fetish in mine, I knew what I must do. I tugged the equally warm prodigal ring from my bag, and deposited it carefully in her open palm. As if from a distant earthwalk I heard myself say, "If this ring can find its way home, so can we all."

Now, looking back on that moment, I realize that a chord was struck within me; a coming together, a gentle untethering in the sound of a heartbeat.

I was coming to see the potential that opens for us as we embrace finalities. I was coming to understand that trusting the process in concert with paying attention leads to a new level of perception and awakening. Then things seem to sort themselves out, find their places, and balance.

And, oh what a joy it is to discover that when you relinquish that which you prize, things of even greater significance appear.

"Dwell as near as possible to the channel in which your life flows."

Henry David Thoreau

Potentiality

In the dance of life, one thing inevitably leads to another in a chain reaction of coincidence and consequence. Leaving the town of Zuni, I was especially mindful of the phenomenon of unfolding. I was especially mindful of possibilities.

As my furry friend and I bumped along across Route 264 towards Window Rock, Ganado, and the mesas of the Hopi lands on our way to Sedona, Arizona, I was perceiving an emergence—a tempering—even a metamorphosis. Indeed, the very scene before us augured change. Giant saguaro cacti arose from scrub, to paint living hieroglyphs against a sky shading from azure to magenta. For hours, the shifting colors emblazoned their presence upon my consciousness, as the artist within me celebrated the unbounded energy of the place — and a shift in "vision."

The western horizon called the sun home. It was very quiet now, and chilly. A hawk circled above, and I felt a majestic emptiness within my being. Now, a family of cottonwood trees beckoned us to the side of the road, where, snuggled up in a traveling blanket next to that nice warm dog, who seemed to know my every notion, I enjoyed profound inner stillness. Here, in these ancient lands, I sank into sleep like a child at its mother's hearth and when, hours later, I awoke to gaze on a full moon, and hear the distant baying of a wolf, it was as if for the first time. Somehow the exchange at Zuni had released me to know freshly and in new ways.

I began to recognize the **experience** of an all-at-once, nonlinear, almost fluid awareness. Here, all manner of things become possible. "Oh, if only there were a way to share this feeling with every person in the world," I wished.

I have listened for the spirit voices,
I am weary, weary from my search,
I sleep among the willows,
While the changing woman
Cradles me, cradles me.

Lara Lavi
Songcatcher's
Dreaming in Color, CD

Sedona: Pure Potential

*D*awn. Filtered sunlight. Crisp air. Frozen dew drops. The canyons buzzed with Life. Sedona, Arizona carved her way into one of these just around the curve. Maggie and I had departed our night's lodgings in Flagstaff (just thirty miles away), to navigate the serpentine route through the Oak Creek Canyon and Verde Valley in order to be in Sedona in time for breakfast. A small cafe' soon crept into view. Adjacent to the café, an interesting rock shop caught my eye. "Hmmm!" It looked perfect for a minor league rockhound (like me) whose Grampaw had taught her about fossils and mineral formations, and in the process had passed on his taste for treasure hunting.

Grampaw and I had relished finding many colorful glinty, geometrically shaped crystals; and we had always anticipated the uncovering of the "one" as yet undiscovered. So, on this day, with inherited zeal, the goal was to perpetuate the legacy of "The Search", the quest for a true rarity. I was primed. After Zuni, I expected the unexpected. I *expected* bounty!

Still riding serendipity's wave, and forgetting all about breakfast, while Maggie settled down on the back seat, I entered the rock shop. A pretty woman of perhaps thirty emerged, all aglow, from behind boxes of stones, some containing huge rough chunks and others full of smaller polished pieces. Her smile was friendly. Something in it reminded me of those I'd found in Zuni. Maybe it was the openness. We connected right away talking about rocks and minerals, treasure hunting, travels, and good fortune. This was Joan Marie, who also was a rockhound. Whenever she got the chance (which wasn't too often these days since her own business was flourishing) she helped out at the store. That way, she explained, she got to meet the miners who supplied it and to have a first glimpse at their finds. She knew much more than I did about mining, that was for sure, and I also discovered that she knew much more about crystal formations. She saw these as representative of a universe of order.

She had recently understood this quite clearly, she confided, when she realized that crystals, indeed all things in the Cosmos, are sustained and organized through attraction forces. I had observed how crystals grow in water. What she said made sense.

"How did you figure this out?" I asked, and was told that she'd had a "shift in awareness" that seemed to flow from the process of opening up to an extended sense of perception in a nonverbal, nonlinear experience she had discovered called Reiki. This left her mind exploding with the possibilities of a world, interconnected, and evolving itself through loving attraction.

"Reggae," I repeated, thinking how odd it was to have come to such numinous conclusions while dancing.

"No, no, not Reggae," she laughed uproariously, as if tickled to her bones, "Reiki, Ray-KEE." Without giving me a chance to get a question in edgewise she continued...

"You know," she said brightly, "knowing that we are absolutely, always, at every moment, connected in a natural process inspires me! I like swimming in a sea of energy, knowing I "am" it... knowing I have never been apart from it even when I think I am... knowing that the separateness exists only in my mind... nowhere else... knowing that the separateness is an illusion..."

"Well, I'm not so sure about that!..." I interrupted, but was firmly told -

"This is based on fact, not on my philosophy or hoping or dreaming! Science, quantum physics, general systems theory, astronomical theory, and mysticism all confirm that we are part of one vast universal chain of being - from the tiniest rose quartz crystal to the most distant star in the spiraling galaxies..." and her voice trailed off wrapped in wonder... and I got my chance to slip in my question -

"What's Reiki?" I asked meekly.

Now Joan Marie was just as clever as my special Zuni ring. She wound her way around the subject until I was fairly bursting with curiosity.

"Ya' know," she mused, "I think that our problem is that we've just plain forgotten the Law of Concentrated Focus and so we've

"My desire for knowledge is intermittent; but my desire to commune with the spirit of the universe, to be intoxicated with the fumes, call it, of divine nectar, to bear my head through atmospheres, and over heights unknown to my feet, is perennial and constant"

Henry David Thoreau

also forgotten how to tap into Pure Potential!"

   "What on God's Green Earth are you talking about?" I asked, puzzled.

   "Oh!," she grinned, looking directly into my eyes, "would you like me to explain Reiki to you?"

   *A*fter yesterday's drama, I was open to appreciating whatever the universe had to offer. And curious. With another round of questions and answers, I discovered that Joan Marie and her husband were licensed therapists who had a practice there in Sedona. They specialized in "stress reduction therapy for wellness." To **experience** Reiki, she explained, required only that I bring myself (wearing comfortable clothes which were to be worn throughout the session) that afternoon to their studio where I would discover something akin to a gentle touch massage, which would be deeply relaxing.

   Was it just a coincidence that I had happened upon Joan Marie on this trip of fortuitous detours?

   What do you think?

   She had offered me this opportunity to **experience**, first hand, a new way to Relax– just what I was looking for—Reiki: it sounded promising. Opportunity, in the form of a treat!

   "I accept!"

Vessels

Deep
into vast canyons
our winged shadows glide
like eagles soaring...

Borne up
on waves of sound
and light
detached from earthly moorings...

They are renewed.

Then from pure emptiness
into the vessel
of bone and flesh
Life breathes her sweet pourings

And shadows fly Home.

Earth Mother,
enclose, embrace, entrance us with your beauty.
Welcome us to your expansiveness.

Motherhood is full of implications.
Will you teach your children, soon?

Wind-in-the-Feather

Reiki and Relaxing: Creative Potential

*J*oan Marie's studio was a tribute to rock lovers, plant lovers, and lovers of sound and scent. She had created an environment using nature's tools, which was soft, comfortable, and warm. Reclining on a cushioned table, and putting aside my "agenda," I began to notice a welcomed easing of tension in this hospitable space. Joan Marie had just completed her "First Degree Reiki Training," and seemed very pleased to have found a candidate so open to, and interested in her discovery. Little did she know the level of anticipation I had reached. I was exploring foreign territory, far, far from the "normal" confines of the corporate comfort zone. This was mysterious stuff— one degree beyond the norm.

Intrigued I was, but, with this, my very first **experience** with Reiki, my interest changed to astonishment. As I closed my eyes and she commenced the session, I began to *see*, (with inner-sight) the vivid colors of yesterday's drive across New Mexico, intensified. Next, the emotional magnitude of the whole day's experience touched my heart once more, and I was mindful of the moment, then…and now…and again. This "extended sense of perception" was new to me…What did it mean?

Joan Marie had placed her hands just above my eyes, then, after a few minutes, moved her hands to the right and left of my temples. As the positions changed, time melted. *I relaxed, deeply.* With the deeper, slower, breathing came the thought… "our essence is energy…". When the hour (*a whole hour?!?…*) had slipped away, doubt had departed. I felt terrific! This, I expressed, gratefully.

Joan Marie smiled and said, "My Native American friends refer to the feeling of connectedness in Reiki as 'Itaki' or 'Spider Medicine' - the golden web that connects all things. Reiki gives us a wonderful opportunity to see how this can be so."

"If you feel drawn to the experience," she suggested, "go ahead and look up a Reiki Master and learn to practice Reiki yourself… you might find **your hands have eyes of their own…**"

Elements

Earth
Air
Fire and
Water
Seek justice through
Simplicity and
Reverence.

They need Us so!

Wind-in-the-Feather

A Path to Relaxation

*W*e live by the water in the Great Pacific Northwest. An island in Puget Sound is our home and it is to this shore we return, time after time.

After a long assignment back East and three weeks on the road with its many fortuitous detours, it was gratifying to sight the "homeplace." The Pacific Northwest is famous for forbidding, lingering mists, and gray winter skies. Yet, on that moonlit December ride, as the ferry glided silently between islands, the holiday lights of Friday Harbor reflected a bright mood in the black waters, which I could "feel" to the depths of my being. We had arrived home safely—with gifts for our Island friends. Peña prints. Southwest artifacts. Bear fetishes. A few doorstoppers, in the form of polished rocks. There were wonderful stories to tell, and there was even a special present from Joan Marie, for me a gift certificate for another Reiki session!

Within the week, I touched base with a Reiki Master of *The Usui System of Reiki*. Willingly venturing one degree beyond the norm this time, I stood on the threshold of discovery with enthusiastic expectations. I was aware of that "glow" I had come to know as she listened to me talk of happy accidents that led me to her doorstep. I asked her many questions, and was impressed with her wholeheartedness. Here was a seasoned professional, an R.N., with a Masters Degree in Medical Social Work, who had been teaching Reiki for years. She explained that her "teacher was Phyllis Furumoto, who was initiated by Takata, * who had been taught by Hayashi, who was the successor of Usui, the Founder!" I gathered that this was her lineage. Obviously, she was proud to share it with me.

"Reiki is a gift you give yourself," she said. "The practice assists you in cultivating your own ability to attune to your own physicality and energetics through initial, and then more specialized trainings called 'First' and 'Second' Degrees. If you invest yourself in the practice you will find that this not only relieves stress, and promotes well-being, but can give you a whole new perspective on the meaning of life!"

See Appendix A, and Suggested Reading

"I guessed that," I replied, confidently.

She invited me to attend a weekend seminar, during which I would receive training in the initial practice, and my First Degree Certificate. (Details later.) That sounded fine to me, but "what about Second Degree?" I asked. She laughed gently, and said, "Oh, my goodness, don't be in such a rush! It takes time to assimilate this training! You are moving into *"Energy Medicine"* here, and there are learning curves and adjustment periods just as in any other discipline or artform. As a matter of fact," she continued, "our professional association officially recommends that you wait a minimum of several months."

Obviously, there was more to Reiki than I had suspected. So, for now, I would try "First Degree Training". I would consider her advice and wait to see if I wanted to go further.

My business pals in Boston, Detroit, Chicago, San Francisco and Seattle, firmly inured in the competitive (subject/object) business view, had assured me that "Relaxation" was of great interest to them, but had forgone "doing something about relaxing." When I told them of my upcoming training and of my initial **experience**, they wondered if it was all just "too good to be true." But, my intuition told me that my optimism was valid, and that the upcoming Reiki seminar held exciting prospects—for us all. My first Reiki **experience** had shown me great possibilities.

The very next weekend found me ferrying to neighboring Orcas Island for the weekend seminar. Rain poured down in massive, strident, clattering sheets, but inside the log cabin where Takata herself had once stayed, a fire was burning in the stone fireplace and it was warm and dry. A medical doctor, an author, several nurses and two computer "nerds" would be taking First Degree Training with me, as we all began climbing an alternative ladder to relaxation. And so, even though it still seemed a bit strange and mysterious to one who generally wore business attire and carried a brief case, I trusted the "happy accidents" that had brought me here. "What can transpire," I wondered, "when one dares to explore just one degree beyond the apparent?"

"When the mind stays serene, whatever happens to us is good."

Rainer Maria Rilke

Just for the Record

*T*he field of Industrial Psychology has paid particular attention, in recent years, to statistics regarding the correlation between employee effectiveness and stress. Research indicates that those who choose to ignore the physical and nonphysical signs of pressure, get sick more frequently than do those who know how to alleviate stress. This is a familiar concept. However, upon completion of initial training in the Reiki methodology, the stress/disease connection often becomes clear in *a new way*. This is not about remote statistical analyses—this is about taking personal responsibility for wellness at all levels, being open to viewing your relationship to your environment in *wholistic* ways, about accepting the notion of *global wellness* as something directly related to you! You do not have to be a rocket scientist to know that statistics say that it is smart to employ some regular relaxation practice. You do not have to be a genius to figure out that the Reiki experience puts you in contact with a different perspective. It just is good common sense to include the practice in your everyday life-style; it offers far-reaching possibilities. Amidst the myriads of stress management techniques, I had stumbled upon one with which I felt at home and which I have practiced every day since that first class. With this practice has come a new sense of inner, and outer balance, and a new outlook on life. First Degree Reiki Training proved to be a window of opportunity for relaxation, and creative inspiration.

When you create a comfortable space for yourself and you expect a quieting, you engage a *process*. You set in motion a dynamic that releases tension, and can bring about, and sustain, a sense of improved mind-body-inner-spirit integration. You are activating your own natural healing mechanism! You feel good…at home with yourself in the universe.

Think of it. Reiki training and practice helps you to connect with the best things about yourself—reminds you of your "resplendent personage." To the extent that you allow it to happen, you can open to your potential as both a physical and energetic creature. Then tautness, on many levels, slackens, as you come to a new appreciation of your competence and vitality. This works synergistically to create positive momentum towards undoing tension all around you. Your dedication to the practice of Reiki has big rewards... if you *set foot* on the ladder.

"Oh, what a catastrophe, what a maiming of love when it was made personal, merely personal feeling. This is what is the matter with us: we are bleeding at the roots because we are cut off from the earth and sun and stars. Love has become a grinning mockery because, poor blossom, we plucked it from its stem on the Tree of Life and expected it to keep on blooming in our civilized vase on the table."

D. H. Lawrence

"I am for those tiny, invisible, loving human forces that work from individual to individual, creeping through the crannies of the world like so many rootlets... which, if given time, will rend the hardest monuments of human pride."

William James

Your Experience Counts!

As you "connect the dots," what "fortuitous detours" led you to explore just one degree beyond the apparent?

Your Fortuitous Detours:

When:

Where:

Why:

How:

Expectations

Please note your expectations in the following areas.

Your General Expectations:

Physical Expectations:

Mental Expectations:

Emotional Expectations:

Relationship Expectations:

Inner-Spirit Expectations:

Energetic Expectations:

About Reiki

3

Expanding Journey

If you
Put aside
The Ladder of your Discontent to
Step forth, trusting
Upon the Path that is a spiral,
Leading to the other Paths which
Curl their way with yours -

In and Out -
Until your journey expands,
Through interweaving,
Will you not reach "Beyond"?

Wind-in-the-Feather

"...a great change is stirring..."

Hawayo Takata

Ladders and Perspectives

A motley crew of assorted backgrounds and corporate career paths assembled. We were ready to make a personal investment in some form of relaxation. The meeting place was a small conference room on the third floor of the office building where we all worked. It was equipped with an oblong table, a dozen chairs, and an overhead projector. This grey-toned inner room buzzed with the sound of fluorescent lights, and possessed the aura of a dank cell. There were no windows, fresh breezes, or bird songs to distract or remind us of our living story. A plastic water jug sat on its tray in the center of the table, surrounded by white polystyrene cups...offerings on the Altar of Consumer Manipulation.

We were a small group with a strong desire in common, which together with our lifeless meeting space fired our enthusiasm for opening up an alternative for releasing *tension*. There were other methods of varying value (exercise, "downers", martinis, escapism, counseling…) but we were looking for something simple. Thus, on that day just about a year after my initial Reiki Training, I had prepared an informal talk at the request of the group. This was something I had anticipated with delight.

As this minor assemblage convened, I introduced an odd-sized piece of furniture to the room. It was of standard height for a chair, but had dips, curves and holes in it… and was accompanied by a visitor from the outside… a Reiki therapist! "Show and Tell time!", I chortled, ready to share what facts I knew about Reiki, and the experience. Those interested in a "hands-on" demonstration wouldn't have to go far.

Now, ten years later, and a Reiki Master (teacher of Reiki) myself, I am honored to share this information with you! This is the subject of the chapter that follows. In this chapter we take a look at some of the most frequently asked questions about The Usui System of Reiki. (These questions are set out in the margin.)

Questions

1. *How can I locate a Reiki Master?*
2. *Who teaches the Reiki methodology?*
3. *Where will I find the right teacher for me?*
4. *What should I expect from such a teacher?*
5. *What is the point of regular Reiki practice?*
6. *What is the conceptual basis of Touch for soothing within Reiki?*
7. *Who practices Reiki?*
8. *What does Reiki Training cost?*
9. *How does the Reiki methodology compare to other techniques?*

About Reiki Touching

*W*hat is your first instinct when you twist the wrong way and feel a twinge of pain? "Yikes!" you sputter, and put your hands on the offended spot. And when your little child is feverish, do you not instinctively place your hand gently upon the child's forehead? When loving folks meet, they touch, hug, hold hands. You have probably noticed how dogs, cats and all sorts of furry and feathered creatures poke, prod, nuzzle and touch. *It's just natural.*

Ashley Montagu, prolific writer on all facets of human development, says that, "The communications we transmit through touch constitute the most powerful means of establishing human relationships, the foundation of experience." He points out, too, that, "...the need for body contact...may become intensified during periods of stress." Indeed, in a simple touch so much transpires! Concern, caring and healing all are conveyed. This is what Reiki touching is about. When these messages are conveyed, our response is to relax... and to open to new possibilities.

Reiki touching is a *natural* and simple response to any number of circumstances. It is important to note that these circumstances involve an exchange of/or a shift in energy. The practice of Reiki may give you a new perspective on the act of touching. You are initiated through this experience into a new understanding of what your role can be as an instrument of change for yourself and others. You may glimpse the integration tendency (the action of healing) we all possess called "healing". You may even experience a wholehearted sense of your at-ONE-ment with the cosmos.

In Reiki, we seek to become catalysts attuned to subtle energy—that which sustains life.

The Reiki methodology is a straightforward and simple technique of balancing and transferring energy. It is not difficult to learn. In the act of learning Reiki you become like both the guest and the provider of a banquet of life-affirming delights. You empower yourself as a living being interconnected with other living beings in a vibrant energy field to nurture yourself and others.

"I remind myself that my inner and outer life depends on the labors of other men, living and dead, and that I must exert myself in order to give in the measure as I have received and am still receiving."

Albert Einstein

About Finding a Teacher
"When the Student is Ready..."

*Y*ou may have become interested in the practice of Reiki because you *experienced* it. You may suspect or realize that it is an effective tool for tension relief and for processing stress. Soon, however, you may come to find that Reiki offers more than this.

As Sharon L. Van Sell, R.N,, Ed.D., mentions in the February, 1996 issue of <u>RN Magazine,</u> Reiki generates strong testimonials from patients with AIDS, lupus erythematosus, chronic pain, and a host of other conditions. She goes on to mention that double blind, randomized clinical trials and lab reports confirm the positive results. Says Van Sell, "Whether you (nurses) work in an acute care facility, or attend patients who need long-term care, Reiki therapy gives you the tools needed to minister to physical, emotional and spiritual needs."

If you have had a memorable Reiki *experience*, or, through on-going therapeutic sessions have come to enjoy Reiki's potential for alleviating stress, you may want to learn this methodology for its energizing, integrating, or healing effects. The time may even come when you will want to explore deeply into the practice. In any case, please consider this wise advice: One of the first requirements, if one is interested in commencing or continuing the study of *any* artform, is that "one finds one's own teacher." So it is with *The Usui System of Reiki.*

Remember your favorite teachers throughout the years... those you liked, and respected, and who took a personal interest in you? In your pursuit of Reiki, look for nothing less than this! Do not compromise! Do not settle for second best! Honor yourself by looking for one who is genuine, for that person may become a gateway for you. Ask difficult questions of this person. Ask about your prospective teacher's philosophy, Reiki experiences, and how long it took this person to become a Master.[*] What aspects of mastery does this person demonstrate?

"The Master gives the student nothing he or she does not already have, nor does the Master take away anything that is not already absent."

Phyllis Lei Furumoto

*See Appendix A

Since there are many Reiki Masters (some of, and some not of *The Usui System*) all over our globe finding *a* teacher is not a problem. What might be challenging is connecting with *the* one for you. In this sense, your search may be quite arduous. It could discourage those who lack stamina or enthusiasm. Over the years I have come to see that only those who are really drawn to any artform delve into it — and Reiki is no different. Really wanting the understanding is probably what ensures success in connecting with a guide and mentor.

*O*nce you have found *the* teacher, you can easily learn the Reiki Methodology. Then, you will be pleased to find how neatly this relaxation practice blends into your daily routine. You can tailor it to fit your individual needs. You can share it. You can present yourself with a simple, readily accessible focal point for dissolving stress and for attaining new perspectives, always no farther removed than your fingertips. This may unfold into an avenue for exploring and developing your innate resources. Interestingly, as they say: "When the student is ready, the teacher will appear."

In the meantime, keep your eyes and ears open, do some research and follow your inner guidance. Many people have participated in Reiki relaxation over a period of time before taking the Training themselves. Some folks prefer to continue with Reiki as participants (as opposed to practitioners) and that's just fine. You see, in cither case, you can experience "energy medicine," and thus touch-in to a new sense of your real connectedness with an energetic system. In this experience, an alternative way of perceiving and negotiating in both the physical and energetic worlds opens to you.

About Costs

A program of Reiki therapy in which bi-weekly or weekly sessions focus on relaxation may be on your agenda. If so, the costs will be in the range of $30 to $50 per hour. Most therapists work on a sliding scale and are open to making arrangements. Should you be interested in the investment necessary to take a Reiki Training Seminar, the following information might interest you.

The founder of the Reiki methodology, Dr. Mikao Usui, felt strongly that unless there was an *energy exchange*, ("energy exchange" in this case, equals bartering, services, or paying money) what happened as a result of the Reiki *experience* could be undervalued. We do not give Reiki training away. Reiki training is not free, but the cost for training *is* reasonable. Fees represent, first: the desired energy exchange; second: a level of mastery and commitment to the human and living community; and third: (in the case of training for Reiki Masters), dedication to the work and teaching of Reiki expressed in years of additional study and training in a mentored relationship with a Master.

In the Buddhist tradition a ritual of honoring harvest existed. The peasant would bring a bowl of his finest rice to place at the feet of the ancestor who oversaw the harvest. This gift was not the dregs, but the most excellent portion which he "offered back to his heritage, to the earth, and to all that is." Similarly, *The Usui System* views the energy exchange as an honoring process. "Honoring" could include any number of your valued services or bartered goods, or money viewed as "concretized energy."

In this exchange, we are affirming a practice of *being* in abundance, self-empowerment, and of commitment to engaging Life.

$\mathcal{A}$s the Reiki methodology grows in popularity, so grow the discussions (even hot debates) about money! You will find that Reiki Masters of *The Usui System of Reiki* focus upon the *potential to manifest a creative view that encompasses one's natural inclination towards abundance.*

Time and expense issues arise no matter where one lives. The following is an e-mail correspondence forwarded to me at my homeport in the Pacific Northwest from my friend, Sergio, who is a Reiki Master in Italy. Sergio is responding to a request for information from an individual who says… "I would really just like to know why the costs are so high, especially for something like this that is supposed to be a gift to all mankind."

Sergio's Letter
"Reiki is a Big Thing"

About your questions about Reiki, my position is a little different from yours.

First, I personally wouldn't go to a 'weekend course in which all three levels take only three days.'... I feel that Reiki is a serious thing. I cannot think it possible to summarize the experience that one can have in many years of practice in three days.

Would you come, for example, to an intensive course of the Italian Language all done in three days? If so, please let me know. I could ask a little amount of money for it, about 200 US$. And I know Italian very well, so I think I can give you many inputs about my mother tongue!!!

But, how much could you get from me? Are you sure you could receive all my inputs correctly and that you can assimilate them in three days? If so, you could come to my town, Bologna. Here there is the most ancient University in the western world, and maybe we could ask if they can give you (academic honors) after my class...

Frankly speaking, I don't think such a course could give you the experience needed for Mastery. What can you Master after three days? A car? A Lear jet? Maybe a bicycle, in three days, but could you teach it to anyone? A Reiki Master should be someone who knows how to handle Reiki, and who knows how to teach it. Do you think you to be able to do so? Please, forgive my English, I try to speak it since I was nine years old, singing nice songs and playing my guitar, but now that I'm 41 I cannot use it well like you. I think it's a matter of experience and of practising. Like Reiki.

The reason why the trainings of Reiki cost a lot, is that (IMHO) money is something we are attached to a lot. If we can lose a big amount of money in order to become a Master, maybe we have the right attitude towards Reiki. We can do a big effort to achieve the Mastery, because we feel Reiki is a Big thing. We could sacrifice a lot to live with it.

"First, there is a right attitude in the heart..."

But first money isn't the first thing, in my opinion. First, there is a right attitude in the heart, for me Bodhicitta attitude. This is a dharma word (Buddhist). It's the attitude to help all sentient beings. Or to help as many people as possible, to stop their sufferences. Reiki for me is such a tool.

Then there is the experience, and only a Master who knows you can decide if you achieved the right experience. I think that it's not possible to evaluate a candidate to the Mastery through an advertising on a newspaper. It is true that Reiki enhances the sensitivity..., but I feel I have to know the candidate to the Master a lot, before training her/him for Mastery (teaching).

You quote Buddha and Dharma teachings. Generally, Dharma is free, but you have to pay something for the organization, the offering to the Lama, or the Teacher, or the Monks. When you achieve an Initiation you pay for the class, and you generally don't think to it like a movie ticket, but as an offering to the Center instead. I hear that in the past people who were willing to receive an initiation, were asked to offer also their lives to their Gurus.

Even if these things are quite a little different, I feel the motivation inside, is the same. Are you ready to offer your life to Reiki?

If you're ready to spend $150 US, you can learn the first level. It will help you during your entire life, it will change your inner attitude towards people and towards life itself. It'll introduce in your habits a sweet moment of your daily life. It'll soften your enemies and your bad moments.

And it will give you back much more than you spent.

About Training

*F*ocusing attention upon and activating the potential for stress relief is a side benefit of Reiki Training. However, in the larger picture we see that, at its best, Reiki training can introduce a new way of looking at the world - a wholistic worldview.

In the Reiki I Training Seminar (usually taught in four, three-hour sessions) we approach an awareness of our relationship to the whole very simply. Class participants familiarize themselves with Reiki movements, consisting of methodical hand placements. Soon, in a participatory segment of the training, a sense of the artform and potential of Reiki may emerge.

First Degree Reiki Training incorporates the telling of the story of the originator of the Reiki methodology, Dr. Mikao Usui. This story models the integration of Reiki into one's life. The weekend class focuses on the physical dimension of the human being. Correlation of hand positions to various important "message centers" of the body is taught. (There are numerous positions, each directing attention to the body's vital areas.) Later, devotees may discover how the practice of Reiki induces relaxation on multidimensional levels, but for now the basic seminar lays a foundation of format and form.

A Reiki II Training Class, (which usually takes place in two sessions), is specifically for those who have reached a certain level of dedication and commitment to integrating Reiki, and its abundant blesings in a wholistic way into their lives. These practitioners, having come to see the interconnected nature of all living beings, resolve to share with the community, local and global, the on-going practice of the artform. Second Degree instruction addresses a system for furthering mental, emotional and the higher orders of awareness, which invites tranquillity and wholeness into the life process. Individuals now demonstrate readiness to interact with a field of energy that extends out in space and across great distances. They are willing to participate in global nurturance and tension mitigation through contemplative focus,

"I was getting ready - but did not know it."

Wanja Twan
In the Light of a Distant Star

and to deepen their connection through their Reiki practice.

We have come to see that when an artform or tradition begins with emphasis exclusively on the technical, and centers its energies around procedure, it can get distorted, even trivialized; then the artform (even Reiki) can lose its meaning, and is rendered of less consequence than the procedure. Hence, a methodology of power is apt to emerge; a methodology that is subject to forgetting or denying the simple *experiencing* of the artform. This type of activity (which is not simple), glorifies procedures and underplays the very important ripening process that is the fruit borne from awareness, reflection, and commitment. We may risk this eventuality in unmentored training, or in training that mistakenly focuses upon the "doing" (as opposed to the "being") (even in Reiki.)

That is why, just as preparing a gourmet dinner may be best learned from a chef, Reiki instruction calls for interaction with a qualified "coach", who is available on an on-going basis, to act as a guide, and to afford a seasoned perspective. And, that is why when brief descriptions of various Reiki exercises appear later in this text, I respectfully request that you remember that these are not meant to instruct. They are included only as examples of the powerful "beingness" of Reiki.. We hope you find, as we have, that these samples are especially effective in the release of tension. As such, they are not only tidbits of useful, integrative, reflective Reiki, but can be windows to envisioning how we fit in both the a physical and energetic world.

About The Practice, Intent, and Practitioners

*R*eiki is practiced at home, or in the workplace, by persons of all ages and degrees of physical fitness. But it is not practiced as one does a religion. Reiki is very definitely *not* a religion. It is: *Energy — Rei*, Universal Life-force Energy — *Ki*, vibrant energy demonstrated by science to exist in and about living creatures, and a *methodology* brought forward by Dr. Mikao Usui by which we may obtain a new and charged awareness of our physical and energetic realities by directly experiencing both simultaneously. This can result in shifts in multidimensional mind-body states.

*S*ome Reiki practitioners are very spiritual, some are not. And while Reiki, at some levels, *does* encourage spiritual contemplation (even has a mystic quality) the bottom line is *how* you approach it. In other words, a Reiki practitioner may be a Buddhist, Christian, Jew, Moslem, Protestant, Hindu or Pagan. This practitioner may be an architect, teacher, doctor, photographer, talent agent, firefighter, novelist, minister, baseball player, web site designer, violinist, accountant, bookkeeper… you get the idea. No one is excluded from learning and practicing Reiki. Age range is not limitation, nor is sex, body shape or size, talent, intelligence, perceived eccentricities or occupation… but **Intent** *is* essential.

Intent

*O*ver the years, I have come to see that from whatever vantage point we view life, it is wise to take into account how pivotal is **Intent**! Three decades ago IBM researcher, Marcel Vogel, concluded two things about **Intent**.

1.   **Intent** *produces an energy field.*
2.   *Our thoughts and emotions* **affect** *living things around us.*

"Reiki is from the heart."

Mari Hall
Practical Reiki

Intent is serious business. This takes precedence in the practice of Reiki — not who you are, or what you look like. **Intent! Intent! Intent!**

*R*eiki is a standard therapy used in complementary medicine with success. Worldwide, a broad spectrum of practicing health professionals (hopefully, aware of the importance of *Intent*), employ or recommend it including: doctors, nurses, physical and occupational therapists, ministers, chiropractors, psychologists, massage therapists, barbers and cosmetologists. These people are licensed to do "hands-on" body work and use the Reiki methodology in therapeutic environments for all manner of ailments, including acute and chronic stress. (If you are not a licensed health professional, or a minister, you would need to check the laws and certifications in your part of the world before engaging in Reiki as a therapist.)

For those of you who are, or will become certified Reiki practitioners and are interested in sharing Reiki sessions with other Reiki initiates, licensing is not required. A good idea is to hook up with a group of friends, family members or other Reiki folk for exchanging Reiki. In our neck of the woods, such gatherings are called "Reiki Circles". Here endless possibility is celebrated… as in the true story which follows.

The True Story of Ken and Billy

*L*ike many practitioners of Reiki whom I've had the good fortune to meet over the years, Ken was a special guy with a special mission. He wanted to share life's blessings with others. When a group of us got together to discuss the practice of Reiki and to share the experience in the community you couldn't miss Ken. He was a real standout, and not just because of his appearance... I remember clearly that Ken had the countenance of one who is at peace with himself.

This man was a 277-pound angel, who looked as if he should have been a defensive back for the Seattle Seahawks. For all his size, however, Ken was unassuming and remarkably gentle. As I observed him patiently working with folks who were interested in Reiki therapy, I recall how quickly he would center himself, and how sweet was the expression on his broad face. I am thinking now of the night he told our small gathering of a commitment he had made recently and of how that face was etched with compassion as he spoke of a small child who needed assistance. His parents were torn asunder as they watched their little boy suffer... their two-year old was not expected to make it to his next birthday. "You see," Ken explained, "Billy was born with a grave intestinal problem." It seems that Billy's folks were ready to try anything, even alternative or complementary strategies when Ken arrived on the scene. They filled Ken in on the situation. They wondered if maybe Reiki therapy could help, so, when Ken volunteered to assist with Reiki, they said, "Why not?, ... We have everything to gain and nothing to lose."

Ken and Billy's Dad worked on the same construction team. On breaks they discussed the options, the program, and the possible outcomes. Ken explained that it had only been a year since he had completed his initial training in Reiki and that he was somewhat of a neophyte, but that he was willing to offer whatever assistance he could. And so the Reiki sessions were planned and got underway.

Three or four times a week Ken would return from a day of "pounding nails", shake the sawdust from his clothes, get cleaned up, slick down his unruly hair, put on one of his plaid flannel shirts and head on over to visit Billy. Each time the toddler rested in the Reiki therapy, Ken noticed a softening in the tense abdominal area and Billy smiled. Most of this was at Children's Hospital. Billy was not thriving, but at least there were positive signs of improvement and definite pain relief.

The weeks and months went by. Ken kept us informed. He told us how he wished there was something more he could do. The people who came to the Reiki Circle were supportive "distanced" their energy medicine right to Billy, and remembered him in their hearts each week. Now Ken decided that he was ready to deepen his Reiki practice. He had maintained contact with the Reiki Master who had been his First Degree Training teacher. He had just returned from teaching Reiki abroad. The timing was perfect. Ken told us that he hoped that his intentions to deepen his practice, in combination with the instruction and attuning process of the Second Degree Training would open up a way for a breakthrough for Billy. Ken's heart and his stamina for this demanding practice were as big as he was.

If Ken was optimistic, this was not the case with Billy's parents, who after months of anguish and trauma and no miracle cures, were stretched to the limits of their endurance. After the rigors of the invasive procedures Billy had experienced (and would need to continue to undergo) they did admit that Billy's Reiki therapy seemed as comfortable to him as a warm blanket on a cold night. As for the doctors and nurses who had once been reluctant to deposit their trust in Ken's compassionate ministrations, they were discovering an innovative and supportive technique and a new way of looking at their role in the healing process.

Now it had been almost a year since Billy's Reiki therapy had begun. Ken completed his Second Degree Training and continued the consistent sessions with his young client. He reported to our group that he was now "concentrating on higher dimensions, while praying – relaxing and opening to the highest good of all concerned…" Any he stayed with it. Ken knew Billy would improve "without a shadow of a doubt".

But, one day, this mountain of a man appeared at the Reiki Circle with tears in his eyes. Billy's condition had worsened! That evening, we empathized, in unison, and joined as a group (rather like a family) all focused upon loving concern for Billy. Knowing that Reiki can produce a "healing crisis", we released our attachment to the outcome and simply expected that "the highest good of all concerned" would present itself.

When, just a week later, Ken arrived uncharacteristically late at our meeting place, we were filled with anticipation and concern. As he rushed in the door and saw our faces, he began to glow. "Billy's OK! " he beamed. "Something changed this week and the doctors say that if he can make it through this month, the prognosis is good!!!"

That was several years ago, and as of the date of this writing Billy, is alive and well. He is now in elementary school, a vivacious child, who knows all about a "special energy", a great big angel named Ken, and his friends at the Reiki Circle.

On the part of the recipient, or student, and later, on the part of the practitioners of *The Usui System of Reiki*, the primary requirements are few. This is not to say that they are inconsequential. Self-discipline — personal integrity — humility — willingness — a sense of openness to the unexpected or unique — and an adventuring disposition are important. Above all, **empathy**, is mandatory.

As a practitioner, one must be able to learn the Reiki methodology. Confidence grows as the system is used. The ability to sense subtleties, and to intuit appropriate responses is very valuable. Finally, the more balanced an individual is, the more ready to scrutinize "personal negativity" and to move into "personal possibility," the more artful can be the Reiki practice.

As we mature in our process, we expand our perception. We begin seeing situations, events and even physical properties *in new ways*. The more we aspire to the enterprise of climbing the

"Health requires this relaxation, this aimless life, this life in the present."

Henry David Thoreau

We begin seeing situations, events and even physical properties *in new ways*. The more we aspire to the enterprise of climbing the ladder to refreshed awareness, the greater the chances are that we will perceive what we did not notice before.

*M*ake no mistake: with regard to the aspects of Reiki which pull us in... to relaxing, opening, and celebrating Life... in... to new realms of perception, the winds of change **stir from within**, to swirl about uncharted spaces of the multidimensional mind-body, creating unfolding new patterns of understanding and conceptual development. These "new patterns" flourish in a supportive atmosphere.

It behooves the practitioner to be observant in this regard.

"Reiki is a being practice."

About Reiki in a Comfortable Environment

*B*eing "comfortable" is probably one of the most important prerequisites for the practice of Reiki. One of the first things emphasized by our Reiki teacher was getting "comfortable" ourselves before beginning a session. "You *must* be positioned *comfortably*, within and without!", she insisted. So, remember to make mind-body adjustments, loosen-up, and breathe before starting your Reiki session. (This applies whether you are a participant or practitioner.) "Remember," she cautioned, "**the Intent in Reiki is to be a catalyst for *Life-force Energy*, so you must take the time to set your own agenda aside…**"

Reserving a special time and place for the Reiki session, in which you can enjoy a private, undisturbed, "time-out," aids in the revitalizing process. The setting, one in which you feel comfortable is important. Again, this matters whether you are alone, as a practitioner, or with another, as a participant/recipient. As an example, when practicing Reiki alone, we try to lie on a soft surface, dim the lights, close the door, and, as indicated, remove constricting items such as shoes, watches, and belts. When Reiki therapists treat others, this comfortable surface is usually a special table, which is deeply cushioned and covered in soft fabric. The table provides the correct height for the practitioner, who is seated, and a steady, comfortable resting place upon which the recipient can recline.

Whether you are approaching Reiki as a method for enhancing relaxation, physical improvement, mental/emotional issues, or for deeper insight, you will want to pay close attention to your breathing. Breathing * is an integral part of your personal environment, so -calm your thoughts, get "centered," and consciously breathe deeply — concentrating on exhaling fully —then inhaling, prior to the session. Next, seek out a mental connection, through imagery, with a place in which you feel at ease and, again "comfortable" (mine's the "Magic Hammock).

As for a comfortable length of time for a Relaxation session - this is generally fifty-five minutes. This, of course, can vary, as time and necessity permit. Indeed, "unruffling your fine feathers" may happen in a brief, empathic touch, or in ten minutes, (a Reiki Break). Some very distressing concerns respond to marathon sessions, some to daily attention, others to the briefest of gentle Reiki touches. You will quickly come to see this and to recognize your own comfort level and how a shift in awareness portends delicious benefits for yourself, your family, friends, others - for the global community and Mother Earth.

Reiki practice can be beneficial in varying degrees. You may expect minor miracles, or look for more subtle results. Your individual state-of-mind, your belief systems, your objectives, and how much attention you decide to devote to the methodology will influence what happens. Dedication deepens a Reiki practice and broadens desirable outcomes. Some of the first to appear are noted in the following chart.

Features and Benefits of the Practice of Reiki

Features	*Benefits*
• Reiki practice produces *measurable* changes in bodily function.	• Tension relief, noticeable relaxation.
• Involvement in caring for your needs at many levels.	• Heightened awareness, and mental clarity.
• Enjoyment of mutual benefits when sharing	• "Connections", and emotional growth
• Studies show that Reiki helps to balance and ground its participants.	• Lowered blood pressure, and resistance to anxiety.
• Commitment to the practice of Reiki provides time for Reflection	• Insight, abundance, and unexpected blessings.
• Within the Reiki practice, it can become easier to "listen" carefully to body wisdom.	• Pain reduction and preventative care for long term well-being.
• Both problem-solving and flexibility can be by-products of the Reiki . Practice.	• Modification of "old stuff" behaviors, and openness to the new.

"A still mind is one that is free from fear, free from fantasies, free from ruminations over the past, free from concern about what may or may not be happening to it."

Peter Russell
The White Hole in Time

About the Features and Benefits of the Reiki Practice

*A*s you mature in your process, you may come to have interesting new insights directly related to the ***experience*** of Reiki. An energetic model is easier to fathom when one has firsthand knowledge of nonlocal (energetic) space through Reiki. "New" scientific truths of a "new" consciousness are not so disorienting when one is familiar with the energetic territory.

Reiki is a simple way to get in touch with our at-ONE-ment with a vast energetic universe, where, as Thomas Berry, author and Professor at Harvard University points out, "The obvious thing… is that there is an absolute coherence within its total structure and functioning…, (and) we find that this universe is intelligible only in the unity of its being." Reiki practice offers a sense of personal integration into this primary, coherent organic, phenomenon – a functioning universe – a living galaxy – a vibrant cosmos.

Perhaps through our personal experience of Reiki, we may relax into feeling comfortable with becoming (ourselves) agents of change – bringing to the human community a timely transformation of consciousness.

*R*eiki is mysterious.

*W*hen we allow ourselves to "sink in" with it, to soothe and refresh ourselves, we discover that it is also very powerful. But this is not power as we might ordinarily define it. This is not the power of exerting control over ourselves or others, but the power of abundant good wishes—the fruits of the fertile fields of empathy, balance, interconnectedness, and a wholistic view of the cosmos, and our place in it. What greater benefit could be imagined than to become conscious of this special power?

Still, benefits are not *reasons* to do Reiki. *Reasons* could be misconstrued as *goals*. In that case, one could mislead oneself to see the practice of *The Usui System of Reiki* as something at which one *does or does not succeed...* Au contraire! Reiki is a *being* practice!

Although, in all my years as a Reiki Master, I have always seen someone relax with Reiki; if a shift does not happen on schedule, you may erroneously think it is because you are doing something wrong. You may start to doubt the therapist if you are a recipient, or yourself, or your management of the methodology. Do not trap yourself into goal orientation. Standard advice: always simply *experience* Reiki— for its own sake. The results will come of their own accord. Folks generally think that "doing" demands results, so the notion of undertaking something with the intent of *being*, in which "right" is of no concern, can feel unusual. Odd as it may seem, here, *in the practice of Reiki, you will discover that the best way to accomplish anything is to let go of trying to accomplish something.* In fact, in the Reiki session, it is okay to let go of trying to accomplish anything at all!

*R*eiki is a *being* practice, and as such, escapes good/bad, either/or, accomplished/failed, polarized, dualistic thinking. Because of this, it offers plenty of paradoxical potentialities. We have the opportunity to learn, by first-hand experience, that in releasing the expectation ladder, a way opens for the direction and quality of our lives to emerge - towards wholeness - in a Reiki journey into energy medicine.

Usui:
A Reiki Journey
Into Energy Medicine

4

The Core

Princely memories
Swirled 'round in his head
Like so many butterflies bound for
Home,
Fairly astonishing
His eager mind
With joys of places once Known,
Kingly realms,
Music,
Rhythm and Poem,
Until, with half-smile, he
remembered
His Own
Heart's center.

Wind-in-the-Feather

'*I organize in order to nurture,*
Balancing being.
I seal the input of birth
With the rhythmic tone of
equality.
I am guided by my own power
doubled.'

Mayan Verse

"With Reiki, there is always Hope"
                                        Hawayo Takata

"The purpose of Reiki is evident everywhere we look and have our attention.
This is the energy of life, of movement, of essence of everything. It has no
purpose except to be."
                                        Phyllis Lei Furumoto

Can Energy Be Exchanged?

Throughout the history of humankind, whispers from ancient cultures hinted of a body of knowledge involving the transfer of energy through Touch. It was said that this knowledge was very powerful, and so it was closely guarded. Only a chosen few handed it on, from master to student, through the spoken word, until it became mythical.

Still, echoes from time-past-remembering persisted, lending credence to the tales. Were they myth, or did ancient peoples really *use* certain understandings to energize body, mind, and inner spirit; to encourage wholeness, through attuning to life-force? If so, could the knowledge be recovered and shared? This was Mikao Usui's burning question. The account of the manner in which he set about exploring that question leads me to believe that Usui will someday be legendary, for he has an heroic character.

Seen in an Old Photo

It wasn't all that long ago, not hundreds and hundreds of years ago, but in the late 1800's in Japan, that a man of humble origins became well known for his contributions to others. This man's rural family had struggled to provide an education for him. He had attended one of the missionary schools that were common in the outlying villages of his country at the time, and had risen in the ranks of the scholarly community. This same man had the grace to share the moments of his own formation. His stories, his memories accumulated - - memories of a long life dedicated to the pursuit of a burning question - -are bequeathed to practitioners of a methodology based upon his vigilance. He is worth our complete respect. This man was Dr. Mikao Usui.

I cannot emphasize strongly enough my gratitude to this dedicated scholar and humanitarian whose photograph sits before me as I write. If you were to look deeply into his eyes, you surely would discover lights of dignity, civility and grace emanating. Here too, resides quiet good sense.

As I regard this face, I am drawn back to a time in the story of his life soon after he entered a new world of distinctive responsibilities as a teacher at a small university. It was then that Usui found himself routed from his planned path, and experiencing the first reflections of a dawning light in his world. This happened because he was able to relate to those he taught with integrity.

Clearly, Usui could have chosen not to interact with his students, could have avoided the crucial process of relying on his instincts and abilities to give direction to his life, but he was genuinely interested in what they had to say. It must have been in his listening that he discovered a new way of relating (and shared it). Through his practice he (and we) could spend numerous lifetimes without exhausting the possibilities... that practice... Reiki.

Usui's gifts to us come as the result of his interactions - his attentiveness, and a particular experience - - that transformative experience of the heart - - which culminated in a profound awakening.

Good lessons are embodied in his life's story. The truths in these lessons are of a different order from dogma or philosophic statement - (they lend themselves more, I think, to the language of poetry) - yet they invite an awakening, even an evolution of consciousness towards the liberating, the transcendental truths that arrive from earnest striving.

How did this all begin? Well, as you may guess quite unexpectedly. A student's curiosity ignited a burning question for his teacher, Usui, which in-turn led the man to become a student... but let me explain...

The Burning Question

One day, not long before graduation was to take place, a student came to Dr. Usui inquiring... "Do you believe in miracles?"

"Indeed, I do," Usui replied, smiling.

"Have you ever seen this happen?," the student pushed.

"No," responded Usui, now looking closely at the young man.

"Ah," said the student, "For you, blind faith may be enough, for you have lived your life, and are secure. But for those of us who are just beginning our lives, this is not enough. We need to see with our own eyes."

It seemed a simple exchange on the surface, but it disturbed Dr. Usui. You see, in Usui's time, it was not honorable for a teacher to leave questions prompted by the inquiring minds of his students unanswered. Usui felt obliged to amend this situation. He recalled how ancient tales told of miraculous energy exchanges and began to wonder... He knew then what he must do. He *must* climb back in history. To do this he would need to leave his teaching post. Spurred on by integrity and a scholar's curiosity, he commenced a quest that would last for many, many years.

Mikao Usui engaged his fellow teachers in discussion as the student's question continued to rummage around in his mind, but to no avail. He read all the books that he could find and scoured his own intuition, until it finally occurred to him...some stories of miraculous healings had come to his homeland by way of missionaries from the

"Let the beauty we love be what we do."

Rumi

West. Leaving the comfort of "the known" he expanded Western theology and cosmology. This was a starting place, but as his "journeys" continued, he began to realize that obscure, ancient teachings were veiled for a reason. He realized that Jesus, himself, had insisted that who witnessed His healing miracles remain silent. As He sent forth a leper, now cured, He had said, "See thou, say nothing to any man." (Mark 1:43). But who could keep quiet about this kind of news? Human nature was what is was (and is) and that was what Usui was counting on! Almost two thousand years A.D., Usui found himself on a frigid trail. Nevertheless, Usui's persistence could thaw the most icy landscape, and he was well aware of the power of commitment.

Usui now turned his attention to the "miracles of healing" attributed to the Buddha. He immersed himself in the study of ancient Chinese scripts of the Buddha's teachings. Buddhism had come to China and Tibet in an interesting way, he remembered. Buddhism had originated in India, and there the practice was written and taught hundreds of years before it came to China. When the Moslems came into influence, Buddhism, its denizens, and most of the ancient texts were eradicated. While this was going on, the war lords of Tibet - who had no written language - were becoming more powerful… and one of these, seeking political strength, decided his language would have to take on written form.

The Chinese, as Usui recalled, had by then adopted Buddhism. In the process, they had procured the services of monks and scribes to translate Indian texts and were well into the Buddhist practice. So, the Tibetan king followed suit. He collected as many of the Buddhists who were fleeing India as he could, and set them up in Tibet. He demanded that they devise a written language and that they translate ancient texts.

One of these texts was the Lotus Sutra, in which numerous references were made to the Buddha's healing abilities.

The Search for Ancient Knowledge

*U*sui learned Chinese, so that he could read the esoteric commentaries to the Sutras, but found no answers in these texts. He did however discover a striking similarity between the teachings and rituals of *Tibetan* Buddhism and early Christianity. That was interesting!... Now, he concluded that the *Tibetan* Sutras might illuminate him.

Mikao Usui was determined, patient, and willing to put in the effort, and to do the necessary work, certainly a man worthy of respect. Now he proved that he could extend himself one degree beyond even that... he began to take his search on the road... to visit a number of Buddhist monasteries. At each he inquired if any residing there knew of miracles, healings, or cures. "We're too busy with the work of healing the inner-spirit, to worry about healing the body," the monks replied.

Then, one day, as the story is told, when he least expected it, Usui came upon a Zen monastery. This monastery was the smallest of all those he had visited. He had overlooked it before, but within its walls lay promise. There he encountered an old monk whose face was lit with a perpetual smile. He understood the sincerity of Usui's quest. The Abbot, the most senior monk, understood many things the others did not. Immediately, Mikao sensed a kinship... recognized a mentor.

Indeed, when Usui disclosed to this gentle soul that he thought he could not go on, the wise monk carefully reminded him of the Zen saying: "When one door closes, another opens!"

And so, this is how Usui came to see that he must take his search inward. At the Zen monastery, he surrendered himself to the Abbot. In so doing, Usui acknowledged this monk as his teacher and mentor, and became a Student - not a student of the Abbot, but a Student of himself!

Commentary

Dr. Usui was a punctilious scholar. Before translating the Tibetan scrolls, we might expect that he gathered substantial research on the history of energy transfer and the "marvelous deeds of God." Let's take a look at what he might have found.

Evidence of the use of *Touch* for physical release and healing had first come from Tibet, where *Touch*, or "laying-on-of-hands," was mentioned in medical texts dating back to 2600 BC. A systematic set of hand movements, over specific areas of the body related to various organs, was practiced in ancient times. These, too, were recorded in the annals of early medicine.

In the Greco-Roman civilization, healing with *Touch* was a function of many temples, and healing "miracles" were recorded on stone tablets, which somehow were preserved and destined to be excavated in modern times. Likewise, the records of the scribes of Egypt, chronicled the knowledge of hands-on-healing practices. Those records, in hieroglyphics on temple walls and on papyrus, also revealed that the laying-on-of-hands was a customary practice of ancient Egyptian physicians.

In India, in traditional Hindu practice, *Touch* communicated the spiritual union between man and God, producing a spiritual awakening, great comfort, solace and healing. This *awareness of the God-to-man connection* was evidenced in the healings attributed to Christ—the very healings that had inspired Usui's prolonged search and had ignited his quest for illumination.

Indeed, *Touch* is a familiar theme in the story of humankind. In tracing the historical role of *Touch*, we encounter most cultures throughout the world. Cultures of China, Tibet, India, Japan, Egypt, Europe, Eskimo peoples, Native Americans, the aboriginal peoples of Australia, and various island nations all employed (and still employ) its use.

During his years of discovery, Dr. Usui began to understand that the practice of the Tantric Buddhist tradition would provide answers to his quest for healing. Because of his steadfast research effort, he had become attuned to nuances in structure and form, and eventually found certain passages that led him deeper into himself. He read and reread these, at last fathoming different meanings, different connections within himself, and a different way to open himself more...and more...until he was open to receive whatever the Universe would offer him as a gift... "Perhaps the key to spontaneous healing is in an expanded awareness of our *physical* nature," he surmised. And, indeed, after more than a decade of inquiry, Dr. Usui had rediscovered an obscure door to ancient understanding.

However, it is one thing to be able to *understand* how to do something—to fish, to paint, to write.... It's entirely another to be *able to do* what you wish. So, a new question arose: If one understands the *principles*, how then does one allow the *being*? And now the story continues...

The Story Continues...

*T*he Abbot, who was as intrigued by this question as was Usui, suggested that they go into retreat to ponder what lay ahead. Both men would contemplate. Enlightened masters had visited *possibility*, through contemplation, for thousands of years, so it was expected that following their example, looking deeply within their own nature as human beings, as mindful creatures, as explorers, as passive observers, they might tap the depths of wisdom. In deep reflection lay the gateway to transpersonal reality.

Both men sat quietly and rested in their breathing. Finally, Usui's mentor suggested a pilgrimage to the Sacred Mountain. Having come to the same conclusion himself, Usui agreed. And the abbot warned:

"This could be a dangerous journey, Mikao."

"I know, dear friend, but I've come this far… I cannot turn back now!," replied Usui. "If I don't return in twenty-one days, just send someone to collect my bones."

Commentary

Fasting and meditation are, and have been, used by those seeking enlightenment since time immemorial. Contemporary scientific documentation supports what the wise ones of old knew, that brain chemistry changes when subjects fast, or meditate, releasing consciousness-enhancing chemicals. Furthermore, the focusing of attention that occurs in meditation or deep contemplation, seems to organize left-right brain activity into coherent, interacting patterns. This can result in profound awareness, mystical experiences, and a cosmic sense of reality. When the veils of earthly illusion lift, *essence* appears. This is what Mikao Usui, alone on the Sacred Mountain, having *prepared* for this understanding (exhaustively) expected. He awaited a unitive experience. He opened, like the beloved lotus flower of the Sutra, ready to receive.

Twenty-One Days

On this somewhat ominous note, Mikao Usui prepared to go. Like many of us on the verge of discovery, eagerness quelled his fear. Anticipation of a clear vision presenting itself, as he fasted and meditated from his solitary place on the mountain urged him on. Focused in his intent, Usui set out...walking with a purposeful stride from dawn to dusk, carrying with him a goatskin of water and a book of Sutras. As he made his way along the road and approached the Sacred Mountain, a decade of research knocked on the door of Usui's mind. He realized that this was not his mission alone. Others were counting on him. He would remain steadfast, no matter what might happen in the weeks to come, even if his very life were at stake!

Usui took the rigorous climb with zeal. Presently he came to a quiet place, with a single pine tree and an unhindered view, to which a stream flowed. He selected twenty-one stones, then seated himself for meditation; and there began the ritual of the twenty-one day fast, as he placed the stones about him. These stones he would cast aside, one at a time, each day, at dawn.

The days passed, uneventfully, one by one. The shadows of dawn and dusk moved across the mountainside as the sun rose and set. Sometimes a passerby noticed a solitary man, deep in his vigil. Sometimes that man felt the chill night air, or the heat of the sun as he drank the water he had siphoned from the stream. And so it was that the days wore on, and the stones disappeared in six directions, until only one remained.

The dawning of the twenty-first day was very dark. It found Mikao Usui in a trance, with one stone still in its resting spot before him. Then, from the far reaches of his consciousness, there emerged in the still dark sky, a radiant, intense light piercing the heavens, searing toward him!

"This is a test," he exclaimed "I will face it!"

With eyes open wide, he sat still as the light blazed toward him with dazzling brilliance. It did not relent! Swiftly, it struck him between the eyes, bowling him over, and rendering him unconscious.

Then, slowly, a vision began…a vision of millions of colors and rainbows, and iridescent bubbles dancing before him…filling the sky with red…moving from right to left…changing from orange, and yellow, to green, and blue, and purple! The whole sky was now a rainbow! But there was more! As he gazed at the phenomenon, engaging in highest yoga tantric practice of Varjrayana, golden letters representing enlightened understanding of the Sutras—followed one another onto the magnificent canopy above, and presented themselves before him.

At once, he knew, in the deepest part of his humanity, what they were for, how to use them, and that they came from a place of pure joy inside himself. And as he returned to this reality of time and place— to that Sacred Mountain—he knew that his Vision had *manifested a transformation of consciousness.*

To be continued during "First Degree" Training.

"... Crimson gleams of matter gliding imperceptibly
Into the gold of spirit,
Ultimately to become
Transformed
Into the incandescence of a Universe
That is a Person...

And through all this,
There blows,
Animating it,
And spreading over it a fragrant balm,
A Zephyr of Union."

Pierre Teilhard de Chardin

One Degree Beyond

5
The Cosmic Circle

Then chiefs
And sons of chiefs
Upon the waters did reflect,

While one who told the story
Of the People's singing,
Dancing 'round the sacred tree,
Remembered....

And with prayer stick,
To the world of Spirit went,
Wherein there is no time.

Here, drinking from eternal
waters,
Knowing,
Giving thanks,
The wise one flung the stick to
Stream.

"I see the Spirit of the Earth
In each cosmic circle unfolding,
from smallest to grand,
From family, and country
To nations, and tribes,
Blossoming forth from
Mother Earth
Spiraling,
Celebrating
From deep within the
Mustard Seed," she sang.

And Chiefs,
And sons of chiefs in hope and
harmony
Upon the waters did reflect.

Wind-in-the-Feather

On this dusty road
A turtle's crossing is cause
For celebration!

Scott Christopher

One Degree Beyond

*J*t is interesting how things transpire in our lives. Have you ever noticed how you get what you need when you need it? So it was with Usui, and so it has been with me, and probably you! I beg your indulgence now as I take you back once more to "fortuitous detours," and a road which led me to Reiki. Although my discovery was but a butterfly's kiss compared to that of Usui, its unique quality cannot be denied.

As you will recall, my search was for a fresh approach to relaxing in a competitive, intense environment. I wanted to know how to mitigate the effects of stress for myself - and for my corporate clients. Signposts had led me to a weekend seminar on Orcas Island. Those many years ago, I was "getting what I needed," a handy stress-allaying methodology, but I sure was not expecting the gift of an individual like Mikao Usui! Quite frankly, I may not have even noticed him, had I not been *seeing things in a new way*. Yet, it is obvious that his story was/is a model for a singular way of relating to life.

The story impressed me. I think it confirmed something about intent for me, and helped me to solidify my understanding of Reiki as both a methodology, and an artform which held *promise*. There on

Orcas Island, as our teacher wove Usui's tale in the great oral tradition, it was easy to connect with Usui's persistent search and integrity in a visceral way.

Later, returning by ferry to Friday Harbor, a pensive mood overtook me despite rolling seas. I began to see deeper meanings in the story. Winter winds whipped up irregular swells, and green-faced passengers, as we plied our way between islands but, as a result of my earlier experiences, my senses were heightened and even seemed to be fed by the intermittent squalls. Usui's story had stirred something deep within, and I wasn't willing to let go of that feeling. If only I could find something concrete to anchor me to this. On our walk this evening, Maggie and I would search... and that's just what we did.

The elements combined to design a setting which put our senses on alert. Maggie's fur bristled. I was vividly aware of my surroundings. Mists with a timeless quality shrouded the Island in a fluctuating and luminous cloak. Sea sounds and fog horns lent their voices to a mysterious ghostly chorus. Ocean sprays salted the air and flavored it while clouds loomed low on the horizon. As the full moon finally broke through to light the way (and cast shadows all about us) *my* hair was bristling! Here we were at South Beach, one of our favorite "haunts"; and on such a lonely night, I sensed that we were not alone. It was in fact, delightfully spooky...a fine place in which my imagination could play, unselfconsciously.

A century ago, the native Haida Tribesfolk had canoed across the waters of the Straits of San Juan de Fuca, unafraid of the will of the rough currents. They had carried their sick to South Beach to be healed. Most of us had heard about the arrival of their canoes from Old Timers on the Island. "South Beach, 'The Sacred Healing Place'," I mused, absorbing the misty landscape of rocks and logs and dark waters beyond. Neither herring ball nor fishing boat made its presence known on the seas tonight. "If anyone were watching, of what interest could be two pals...merging into a surrealistic landscape ...painted on the edge of the world and time?...." I thought to myself, enjoying the drama.

During the day, South Beach is stunning. It is part of a National Historical Park, once the station of a regiment of American soldiers deployed here, in the late 1800's, to protect U.S. interests during a territory dispute with our neighbors to the north. Wide expanses, then cleared for parade grounds, are now home to a variety of bunnies, who pop in-and-out of their warrens, where the land reaches down to the sea, buttressed by enormous granite boulders. Not a single tree decorates the area; only grasses, in perpetual motion.

By contrast, on a winter night, with mists, sea sounds, and moonlight, South Beach is startling, even mystical!

Maggie and I established an observation post by a huge, damp, old knotty log, washed up long ago at the foot of the towering granite outcroppings. In the summer these were smooth and warm as giant goddess-shoulders, but tonight they appeared as silent, beached sea-creatures.. Poseidon's outcasts.

"This *is* spooky!" I shivered. I was beginning to realize how courageous Usui was, sitting all alone on a mountain with all kinds of *real* hazards and no food for *three weeks*; and I wondered how *I'd* withstand such a test, if mere shadows and mists could affect me so. I cast a furtive look about, half expecting to see the apparition of some Haida chief. In this atmosphere, who knew what might show up? In my heart, I wished for a memento borne of spirit as I cast another sidelong glance down the beach. And that's when I saw it. A shiny object, near the log, caught my eye in the moonlight.

"What's this?!" I exclaimed, as I followed the glint, and with anxious fingers extracted a silver disc from the rocks. It was a charm, probably lost from the bracelet of one of last summer's tourists. (No, no…it really hadn't materialized!) As Maggie prodded me with her curious nose, I held the disc up and the moonlight captured it again. There, in bas relief, were mounted hands, holding a heart. The symbology could not escape me. I was, immediately, reminded of Usui, the strong-hearted man, whose generous spirit touches so many. I tucked the charm in my glove, delighted.

And so it is, that that night—that "cosmic gift"—is not just a memory, but is with me today. The small silver piece has become my mental ladder to what Mikao Usui has come to represent: Openness, Celebration, and Pure Heart Energy - in a Reiki journey just one degree beyond the apparent.

Reflection

Over the years, I've come to see that pausing to reflect upon our encounters as I did that night at South Beach many years ago, has a way of putting things into perspective. Perhaps, finding your own "mental ladder" with Usui's journey into energy medicine will benefit you as it did me.

In a world on the brink of awakening to a new understanding of multidimensional reality; too often we do not permit ourselves the leisure to reflect upon the meaning of this paradigm shift, or "to follow our bliss." Usui's story is a reminder that: It is possible to do this; and—What can happen when we do?!

"Reflection: the transition (which is like a second birth) from simple life to "Life Squared."

Pierre Teilhard de Chardin

21 Questions For 21 Days
A Contemplative Exploration

Consider one question each day. Reflect upon Usui's story. Note your responses.

1. Can energy *really* be exchanged? If this is so, <u>how</u> can it be?
2. Does the effort of exchanging energy have its rewards? Drawbacks? What are they?
3. What challenges *your* honesty?
4. What challenges *your* personal integrity?
5. If you operate apart from your personal, mental, emotional comfort zones, what challenging factors present themselves?
6. How do you react to the long and short term pressure of exploring just one degree beyond the apparent?
7. As you "look within"—become a student of Yourself—and of yourself in relation to the cosmos—what do you see?
8. When was the last time *you* sojourned alone?
9. When was the last time *you* climbed a difficult "sacred mountain?"
10. How far are you willing to go, to honor your inner-spirit?
11. How do you view your energetic and physical dynamic?
12. What's the value of friendship to *you*?
13. What part does sharing thoughts play in your creative process?
14. For you, how doable is a three week "vision quest?"
15. How does the model of listening with your "inner hearing" and seeing with "inner vision" relate to *you*?
16. How may you prepare, as did Usui, to "manifest a transformation of consciousness?"
17. Within the context of an awakened realization of your dual (physical/energetic) citizenship, how would you define "distress?"
18. What was it in Usui's makeup that allowed him to forge ahead with his explorations?
19. How does this relate to *You*?
20. If Usui were alive today how would he see the big picture?
21. If Mikao Usui had something to say to *You*, what would it be?

Try this:

For the next 21 days reflect upon Usui's story. See what happens. It may be a good idea to note your discoveries and thoughts in some tangible way.

21 - Day Contemplation Journal

For the next 21 days consider Usui's story as it relates to your life. Set aside morning/evening contemplation time and space. Note insights, in a special journal, writing a minimum of two pages each day by using the prompters below:

Prompters, points and phrases:

___ scouring intuition

___ the power of commitment

___ willing to put in the effort

___ worthy of respect

___ determination, patience

___ when you least expect it

___ overlooking

___ look deeply

___ mentors and mentoring

___ always possibility

___ fathoming different meanings

___ student of Self

___ Touch, a familiar theme

___ fathoming different meanings

___ pure potential

___ focused attention

___ enlightened understanding

___ place of pure job

___ manifest

___ new "ladders"

___ one degree beyond apparent

___ awakening

21- Day Contemplation Review

Your Burning Question(s):

Your Physical/Nonphysical needs:

Your Challenges:

Your Perspectives:

Your Insights/Sharing:

Your Developmental Possibilities:

Your Personal Integrity:

Your Global Healing:

> *As Pierre Teilhard de Chardin advises, "Reflection: [is] the transition (which is like a second birth) from simple life to "Life Squared." Note the amplifications the past 21-days of reflection have manifested for you.*

*R*eflection can disclose the subtle, the sublime, the "sacred and the profane," if we approach the process as a Student. Asking the question, "What can I learn from this?", implies trusting life. If we are paying attention, Life's a fine teacher!

As one reflects upon Usui's adventure, time and again *new* insights seem to emerge, and discussion of the story seems to produce an endless assortment of responses. Still, most folks agree that the story reveals the wisdom of following your burning desire to find the joy within and the possibilities in life.

That is what happened with Suzanne who was in my very first class as a Reiki Master. I am reminded of the first time I told Usui's story, and of closing by recommending (as I invariably do) that pausing to reflect upon it and to find a memento of Usui, seemed to create an important connection for me.

Suzanne's response is particularly apropos as we consider the practice of Reiki for moving beyond the apparent. It demonstrates how creative *You* can be in releasing great, enormous knots of chronic stress, if you will simply acknowledge the dignities you deserve, the first of which is the timespace to relax and to reflect upon your own nature.

Suzanne has graciously consented to share the following and offers it to You as an example of what can transpire in Your Life, if you so allow...

"To change the modality we must change the metaphor."

Jean Houston
The Possible Human

Suzanne's Story
"My First Encounter with Usui"

"*A* painful stumbling block for me, as I entered the world of Reiki, was that this ancient healing practice was rediscovered by a man, and that men dominated the field of healing in Japan. Mikao Usui is our teacher's hero. I have no heroes, no male mentors. I realize with sorrow that I really don't like men. As a woman, a second-class citizen, I have always felt shame around men and, eventually, anger. Shame that I am not a man, shame that men want me physically, anger that they cannot honor my intelligence. Used by men, abused by men. And yet, married to a man and calling him best friend. Confused? Yes. Sick and aching? You bet. Could this be a major blockage to my healing, this overwhelming negativity towards half of the human race? Why, yes, I think this is something big for me. Sad..

I think these thoughts as I sit on the beach with my sister. The waves move in and out. I look down, there by my shoe is a small tear-shaped gray stone. I hold it in my hand and Usui says to me, 'Cry no more. Hold your tears in your hands and let your eyes see the goodness in mankind.'

I have found my Reiki totem, the hard rocky tear of years of betrayal - my sorrow, rock hard, unyielding, a stone behind my eye, a boulder on my shoulder (now transformed), in Usui's words of healing."

An Interlude

"You deserve a break today…"

Advertising jingle

An Interlude: The Reiki Break

"*Y*ou deserve a break today"… for creative playfulness… for your whole well-being!… a *Reiki Break.*.

A Reiki Break has come to be a favorite of many folks who practice Reiki. It is a planned pause during which your intention is to consider, to focus on, and to relish the possibilities *in* the moment, and *of* the moments of your life. Many Reiki practitioners have come to regard the Reiki Break as an inspired intervention for relaxation.

The Reiki Break addresses coping mechanisms *by re-training your sense of time*. Dramatically speaking, it is a fantastic intermission beyond the timespace realm. It is not ephemeral, though it may seem so, and regal mortals, such as you and I, can enjoy it "to the max" without worrying about over-indulging.

Many forms of deep relaxation can change time perception. These include meditation, chanting, drumming, golf, dance, gardening, motorcycling, or any number of creative pursuits. Although it seems to me that all these are more demanding or strenuous than Reiki practice, all *do* induce altered time perception, where there is a shift in physical awareness, and increased perception of things beyond the physical. These are matters of nonphysical, nonlocal import concerning an energetic reality in which we, as human beings, participate. Current research also indicates that such practices are conducive to intuitive knowing and concept integration.

With the aforementioned pluses, why not just set out for a sunset ride, or plan a daily adjournment to your favorite soaking tub? Good ideas, but the Reiki Break offers you more. In this relaxing interlude you can come to regard the world as present. You could focus your intention towards preventative care. You could attend to chronic or acute situations. You could facilitate the filtering out of fearful resistance to what is before you and the formation of any number of possibilities. There is bounty in a Reiki Break.

If you are willing to set aside fifteen or twenty minutes, you can touch base with your own multidimensional self. You can engage the process of creative fueling, placing yourself in a timespace where exists a qualitative oneness with Nature and Life.

If that is your wish and if you would like a direct *experience* of what can happen when you take a Reiki Break, please try *The 7-Day Reiki Break Time Shifter* that follows. See how you like stepping beyond the restrictive confines of your normal control patterns.

The 7 - Day Reiki Break Time-Shifter

I invite you now to join me at my faorite imaginary spa, where we will just relax into the moment at hand in a spot not found on any map. Directions leading you to this little treasure follow. There is a regime also, and it can benefit you in these ways.

1.   It can help you re-firect your attention towards the possibilities of the moment...
2.   It can remind you to focus on honoring your legitimate ned to replenish your multidimensional self, on a regular basis.
3.   It can be a valuable tool for insight into creative and transformational energy.

As you begin *The 7-Day Reiki Break Time-Shifter Interlude* you will find yourself seeing things in new ways, visiting life in new ways. You may re-discover your native capacity for well-being. You may get back in touch with your love of life and celebrate your place in the entirety of it. Certainly, you already have the tools to do this. At the end of your week, perhaps you will have found new connections with abundant energy. You may delight in feeling very relaxed and together and your admirers may smile at the becoming twinkle in your eyes.

The 7-Day Reiki Break
Time-Shifter Interlude

Day 1: You have heard the story of Mikao Usui. Take a 10-minute time-out for a walk in Nature while you reflect upon what this story tells **you** that is relevant to your life. Note your thoughts.

Day 2.: Take a personal time-out to do, or to find an object that reminds you of what is important to you in the story of Usui. (Try to do this on a walk in Nature). Sit with this talisman, using it as an anchor as you imagine drawing upon the creative, revitalizing juices of the cosmos.

Day 3: This is a 15-minute Break. Think about this as you relax alone in a quiet space. If you cannot fast for 21 days, what would be a good starting place for you? Make yourself a promise to start - wherever that may be. Next, schedule a time for contemplation.

Day 4: Find one more focusing object. Use this to represent your **commitment to yourself to incorporate self-nurturing, creative, and transformative actions into your everyday routine**. Now (very important) assign this object the task of signaling your mind-body to relax quickly into a space of so vast virtually anything might happen.

Days 5, 6 and 7: Begin this time-shifter by exhaling and inhaling for a brief period; slowly and consciously breathing out, counting to an even count (I suggest no more than eight) then breathing in. Seat yourself in an erect, but comfortable posture with eyes on your chosen focusing object remembering its task, in bold above, Day 4.

Days 5, 6, and 7 continued...

Now, breathing out... all the air out of your lungs... push it all out... then taking a deep, cleansing breath in... slowly to the same count, commence your time-out, and a sense of spacious relaxation.

Each day go to a quiet space. This may be outside or inside.

Continue the practice each day of breathing out and in; letting the breath come, paying attention to your breathing until you sense a *shift*.

You are noticing (each day) your thoughts and letting them just float by, and you are now able to feel very relaxed as you continue.

Fold your hands over your heart as you visualize all the stresses and strains you have encountered this day dissolving as if they were part of a fluid stream of clouds dusting by your heart space, and leaving it refreshed.

Imagine a crystal seed in solution growing larger and more complex. See yourself now as a seed in dynamic complexity becoming ordered and in harmony with your "best self."

Open, and *experience* the flow of restorative energy, cascading down from the crown of your head, into the places below... re-organizing, re-establishing balance, and replenishing as it streams... bringing you increased awareness of energetic momentum.

New Perspectives

This page is for note-making. Use it for journaling your daily responses during The 7-Day Reiki Break Program

A. **Your New Perspectives:**

1. **Physical:**

2. **Mental:**

3. **Emotional:**

4. **Relationship:**

5. **Inner-Spirit:**

6. **Community:**

New Perspectives

B.   **I want to explore further:**

1.   **Physical:**

2.   **Mental:**

3.   **Emotional:**

4.   **Relationship:**

5.   **Inner Spirit:**

6.   **Community:**

New Perspectives

C.   **Patterns of tension or distress I see:**

1.   **Physical:**

2.   **Mental:**

3.   **Emotional:**

4.   **Relationship:**

5.   **Inner Spirit:**

"Take a few letting-go breaths and enter the place of inner stillness.

6.   **Community:**

Joan Borysenko, Ph.D.

Part Two

Application

The universe in which we all live is alive! It is a living, breathing energy system of which everything in existence is a part and interconnected.

Most of us, without thinking, believe that our bodies and our surroundings are solid; however, the latest developments in physics have shown that "the body human" and all other objects are composed of living energy. Vast levels of experiments have shown our interconnectedness and our relational aspect as being part of the whole of the universe – and of each other. Therefore, it follows that what affects one affects all.

The Reiki methodology is an ancient art form that allows the individual to tap into the universal energies at "at-ONE-ment."

Keys to an Unfolding Process

6

Tapestry

She looked in the mirror,
And saw behind her
A tapestry

Of sunlight 'midst dancing leaves
Stirred by the breeze
Gently.

And trees, now in full leaf,
Who only yesterday displayed Spring
buds,
And but the day before crackled in
Winter's blow.

She looked in the mirror,
And saw before her
The reflection
In her mind's eye, of dancing leaves,
Stirred by the breeze
Gently.

And knew, all at once, the mirror was
her mind,
The winds of change
But players on it.

Wind-in-the-Feather

---

*"Finally let us not forget that we are in a continuous
relationship with ourselves."*

Peter Russell
<u>The White Hole in Time</u>

Collective Soul

$\mathcal{F}$or twenty years I have worked with a fairly wide range
of people in this country and abroad, and I think it is fair to say that of
the hundreds of people I have met in my journey into *energy medicine*,
none have taught me more than my own students. These self-possessed
individuals, trying hard to live up to certain firmly held principles in the
practice of Reiki, who have a sense of humor about themselves, and a
keen eye for the inclinations of others, who are ever mindful of the
changing seasons of our lives - in the pregnant moments of Earth Mother
- in the empty fullness which leads to liberation - and in the message -
"we must not be selfish, we must share with others," likewise have
shared with me a collective vision.

Our essence is energy.

Just as much as we are creatures of a physical nature, we are
in that measure creatures of an energetic realm. We are thinking,
transcending, transforming beings… distinct as whirlpools in a stream,
yet one with the stream. Or at least, that is what the scientific facts
indicate.

"New thought" is based on the sophisticated awareness of
the potentiality of an imminent and major transformation of

"'New thought' is based on the sophisticated awareness of the potentiality of an imminent and major transformation of consciousness regarding how we come to view the relational aspects of our experience."

consciousness regarding we come to view the *relational* aspects of our experience. There is a fundamental, dynamic aspect in our physical surroundings seen easily in chemistry experiments in which - given just the right combinations of pressure, temperature, proportion and so forth - and with the right catalyst, matter transforms itself from one state to another. This is a reflection of a grander picture. Unity in diversity manifests itself at the higher levels of the dynamic, where interconnectedness, interrelatedness, and other key energy transactions demonstrate that this process follows a pattern and a direction (albeit spiced with mysterious discontinuities.)

So we may venture that universal destiny is written in all that is seen... or is not-visible. It is written in "a code of energetics" for the bold explorer to decipher. Beyond the literal, is an analogical interpretation - which may open to an ultimate, spiritual, even mystical sense of our place in the vastness of creation.

Where does Reiki (the practice) fit in all of this? How is Reiki (the experience) both a direct connection with the physical, *and* an experience of an energetic reality?

Before we go into this discussion, we need to reflect upon the notion that the cosmos is one, indivisible, dynamic whole. It is best understood in terms of relationships and integration. In the Newtonian view, the earth is a composite of discrete parts. Now we are coming to see that the living global community is in systemic synergy—woven, as it were, in a cosmic web which is intrinsically dynamic.

The significance of the practice of Reiki within this context, stems from its power to awaken those deep knowings which feed this important understanding. Knowledge of the facets of the Reiki jewel are illuminated within a process which many say finds its fulfillment in celebrating a new vision of life...

In the following pages, we reflect upon such matters, preparing ourselves for a journey into the heart of a reality that is like a sea of sparkling generative power... *just one degree beyond the apparent.*

Moving Into An Energetic Reality

In every phase of our emotional, aesthetic and imaginative lives we are dependent on our perceptions of the world about us.

We frame an understanding through conceptualization. With regard to the practice of Reiki, for instance, we observe that the conceptual framework is one of balance, detachment from ego, and wholism. This framework is given definition by the integrity of order built-in to the life-process. These are the main concepts which provide a structure through which we can balance, nurture, and refine our consciousness of a "new way" of viewing the universe. Again, as we reflect upon it, we see that these concepts express themselves in the Reiki practice which can become for us a gateway - a *direct experience* of an energetic reality.

There is a great deal that one discovers as one moves into the practice of Reiki. For one attuned, there is much to be unveiled as the months and years go by, and, as mystery becomes mysteriously more mysterious, the artform unfolds. Between the challenge of discovery and the unknown, lies an opportunity for a deeper understanding.

For those who brave the exploration, clues to the experience of a vast, dynamic, unfolding universe appear as, through the practice of Reiki, we commence to expand our universe of discourse. With a new "inner hearing" and an energized "inner sight" we can begin to envision a deeper harmony – a coherent Whole – and within this Whole, our integral relationship to It. But lest we float into the ethers reminding our friends of so many "airy-fairies", let me share a story that will put this all in perspective.

Live life with Passion and Charisma

"The only thing you have to offer to another being, ever, is your own state of being."
Ram Dass

*I*n the years before a back road trip led me to discover Reiki, the bulk of my management consulting practice involved give-and-take with high-performance, get-it-out-there, results-oriented, fast-trackers in marketing-communications-sales. Things were hyphenated-to-the-max around these "win-win" stars, who coped with (or tried to cope with), the pressures accompanying their status. There were those notable few, however, who *always seemed calm.* They seemed to structure their day to allow time for *relaxation.* Everyone relished working with these people. They were leaders with high energy who appeared to derive their comfort not from aggressive competition, but from creative action. Funny thing; somehow they got the message across that *they* knew, that they *knew*, their successes derived from a combination of willingness to recognize-and-move-*with*-opportunity, and the spirit-of-thrill-and-joy-in-life that they embraced. Their message: "Live Life with Passion and Charisma!"

There follows the story of one of these bright lights.

Perceive the World as if
You were a Child...

*N*orm had always said, "Perceive the world as if you were a child." He had the slogan printed in bold italics on memo pads that he handed out to his sales team. It was plastered on the office walls. It was above his door, even on the border surrounding his license plate! It may have seemed a bit odd (if you didn't know Norm) for a guy with an advanced degree in electrical engineering to be so taken with this motto, but it made perfect sense to his staff and to me.

Norm was the manager of one of the "Big Three" automotive accounts for a premier manufacturer of computers. This company (and Norm) hired a good number of senior marketing types through our Search Firm, so I got to know him pretty well over a period of about fifteen years.

Norm had an uncanny understanding of what was being said between the lines, of what comprised a hidden agenda, of moving targets, of consideration, and of uncompromising common sense. He applied his wisdom in the field of business, but he learned it in another kind of field. Norm understood how to tune-in to the energies of Nature. This "added dimension" he employed to the benefit of all in a business environment, and perpetuated as a gift-of-the-spirit to his family and friends, by helping us align with the energetics of the natural cycles of the seasons. At any time of the year this curious pathfinder might be planning a pilgrimage… like the one he organized after the Summer of the Twisters. . . .

Norm had been out assessing the storm damage on the family property shortly after a tornado had ripped through, felling a stand of birch. Norm saw this as an opportunity. He got his sons and wife interested and then the whole family harvested the bark, and engineered, then crafted a canoe which accommodated four people, a dog, supplies and fishing gear. They were reinventing a time-honored family tradition, readying themselves for a "sacred pilgrimage" into the back canals and marshlands of Harsen's Island, a wildlife refuge bordering Lake St. Clair, the smallest of the Great Lakes.

Without mishap, in the predawn hours, maintaining near silence, Norm and the family launched their craft, pushed off with their paddles, and slipped into the fog, imperceptibly. They were paddling their way to a rendezvous with some small mouth bass, and the spirits of the ancestors of the "Grasses Place". Norm's great-grandfather, a Huron, had fished where the reeds and cattails waved. Generations later, Norm knew the exact spot where the Old Man had fished, but not by the grasses alone. He could *feel* it. "What makes a place special is the *energy*," he insisted. What Norm was describing was how, what some folks call, influences, emissions, insights, intuitive knowings, openings or celebrations, bring forth *an alignment with an essential resonance within the universe*. In the same way, recognized the ceaseless patterns of change within a framework of order.

Part of the beauty of the practice of Reiki, just as in Norm's "sacred pilgrimage", lies in the process of teaching ourselves higher skills, by

---

Try this:

Begin observing yourself in nature. Go to a natural area near where you live and see if you can get a "sense of place" - a sense of being attracted to a particular spot. Note your responses.

Try this:

Plan a trip to Egypt (even if it is just in your imagination) When you find yourself at the foot of the Great Pyramid - note your response.

How is this response aligned with Norm's observation… "What makes a place special is the energy…?"

"Part of the beauty of the practice of Reiki... lies on the process of teaching ourselves higher skills, by which we arrive at a place of inner truth."

which we arrive at a place of inner truth. In Reiki, we are both training our mind to stay focused (because it is grounded by a physical task), and moving one degree beyond the obvious to tune-in to a system of energetics. But, let's let Norm pick up this discussion.

The Smirbs

One day when Norm and his eldest son were having lunch at a local drive-in restaurant, Norm got to talking about how "perceiving the world as if you were a child" dovetailed with his personal theories of quantum mechanical physics. Norm always spoke softly when he had some bit of wisdom to share, and he had a habit of starting important lessons with... "Well, let's see...."

"Well, let's see...," Norm proffered to his son, as they concluded a thoughtful talk about their canoe trip to the Old One's fishing grounds... "Well, let's see... you asked me about how I got to know that place by its energy..." and Norm's voice deepened with the confidence he was about to share. "Son ," he nodded, "the first thing you need to know is to pay attention to each place you go." He explained how each place, even the root beer stand where they were that minute, had it's own "aura"... then continued, "and then you have to be able to see yourself as having that same kind of energy- even though it's not physical. Can you do that?", he asked, as his son nodded affirmatively. "If you can," he continued, "then you can also see that you are both solid and three dimensional and beyond time and place."

Seeing his son's eyebrows knit together, Norm reminded him how water could have the properties of a solid, liquid and gas and that we are like that except we are solid, and energy all at one time. Without hesitating, Norm reached for a large recycled napkin from the tray attached to the window, unclipped his pen from his shirt pocket, and began doodling the way he was apt to do...while his son peered over an order of french fries.

"Well, let's see...," Norm murmured, "Well, let's see...there were these two funny little guys called Smirbs (small-time energy beings), one day as they were just being where they were, an energy ball happened to bounce into their playspace." (Norm was drawing cartoon characters ogling a round thing going "boing".)

Norm raised his left eyebrow. "Smirb One (S1) grabbed the ball, and zoom...before he really thought about it, he was showing off, whirling it around his head until it took off on it's own!" Norm's pen was flying now as he scratched out the next scene in short, rapid strokes. "Well, let's see... you guessed it , that ball was out of control...it went boinging back and forth all over the place with S1 in mad pursuit until it boinged right into S2's large nose. It wasn't on purpose or anything, just 'cuz S1 was an apprentice energy being." Norm's face now expanded in a wide grin as he chuckled out loud and looked down at the cartoon Smirbs, and over at his son. "Do you know what happened next ?" he asked. "Well, things got out of hand, there was a chain reaction and S2 revolted, snagging the ball and hurling it right back at S1's nose...entirely forgetting that in the world of energetic reality, where everything is by nature *interconnected*, if you hurt somebody else, you're really hurting yourself.

His son nodded, drinking the last of his soda, but kept quiet. He knew his dad still had something on his mind. And he was right.

"Well, let's see...Hmmm," Norm said gravely... what if S1 = Earthlings and S2 = Earth Mother!?"

"But always, it seems we have a duty to come to greater discernment about our path, about its meaning, about how we walk it."

Beatrix Murrell

Experiencing Energetics, "Ki" Keys

*N*orm would have liked the practice of Reiki. There is grand opportunity here to understand ourselves as beings who are both physical and energetic in nature. There is also the possibility of making a contribution to the "good of all concerned." Participating in the Reiki experience encourages activation of skills you already have. These capacities are agents of change.

I have dubbed these "distinguished energies" the 'Ki'-Keys of the Reiki practice. They strike me as being both "door-openers" (keys), and expressions of energy (ki). They are agents of change worthy of consideration. Each person who experiences Reiki uses different images/words to explain to others a sense of that experience - and the 'Ki'-Keys are my way of trying to share this experience with you. They are not part of the Reiki Training. You may wish to regard them as reference points for navigation about fluid spaces of a new awareness of *being*, and of a new way of seeing yourself as a creature of energy.

1.   Empathic Resonance

*T*he dictionary defines *empathy* as "identification with or vicarious experiencing of the feelings or thoughts of another." *Resonance* is "the state or quality of being resonant." "*Empathic Resonance*" is a term I coined some years ago to describe what happens when you "tune-in" to another living being or, what happens when you do the same for yourself. This special connection, which is nonphysical, can be just as important as a physical intervention. It operates on the same principle as does belief, which can be powered by any number of thoughts or emotions.

Interestingly, all living creatures appear to exhibit *empathic resonance*. The research of Eldon Byrd who was a senior member of the Institute for Electrical and Electronic Engineers, with a master's degree in medical engineering and onetime operations analyst with the Advanced Planning and Analysis staff of the Naval Ordinance Laboratory in Maryland, corroborates this. Byrd, had laboratory access to highly sensitive top-line charting equipment and was able to demonstrate (referenced by Peter Tompkins in his extraordinary book, <u>The Secret Life of Plants</u>), that plants *"exhibit a quality of awareness and empathy to other organisms that are stimulated in their presence."** Byrd attributed this awareness in part to "mysterious mechanics of 'bioplasma' ("Ki"). He noticed a *"change of biopotential* of the cells from outside to inside membrane...", (*italics, my own*), and said, "mutual communication and empathy is the **key**!" (*bold, **his***).

$\mathcal{N}$ow let's take a look at how the experience and works of Dr. Norman Cousins indicate that resonating in a healthy way with others is good for us. Dr. Cousins, while in his prime, was diagnosed with cancer and a was given just months to live. Refusing standard medical treatment he set out on a program of diet, exercise and *empathic resonance.* How did he do this? He did it by engrossing himself in funny old movies. Laurel and Hardy, and others just got him "rolling on the floor" laughing. (Brain and body chemistry alters with hardy laughter.) With this "empathic resonance" change, and healing resulted. Dr. Cousins recovered, and lived, cancer-free, to share his findings. He died at the age of 76! "Belief becomes biology," he said...BELIEF BECOMES BIOLOGY!

"Belief becomes biology"
Norman Cousins, M.D.

Belief becomes biology.

* *See "Suggested Reading" Appendix C*

A Special Connection

$\mathcal{E}$mpathy is the projection of one's own sense of being, and one's own persona onto that of another in order to understand the other better, and to share the other's experience. "Empathy...is not [just] vicarious experience, for it rises from the depth world, and in its most developed form, from our relationship with the Beloved," writes Jean Houston, in Godseed.* "Only through empathy is it possible to step into another's shoes without displacing him or her, or losing one's own identity. (Empathy) releases and empowers the other to become who or what he or she truly is...and thus transformation—be it miracles, healings or new knowledge - can occur. *Anything becomes possible.*"

Empathy is also a gatekeeper of our *interconnectedness* with all living things. This can be observed within the **experience** of the practice of Reiki. Here an infinity of inter-level relations and interactions may occur, just as it happens in the world at large. We certainly do not exist independently of our environment; we both influence, and are influenced by it. As celebrated author Matthew Fox states: "The more deeply one sinks into our cosmic existence, the more fully one realizes the truth that there does not exist an inside and an outside cosmos, but rather one cosmos: we are in the cosmos and the cosmos is in us."

$\mathcal{V}$arious energetic relationships within our interconnectedness express themselves in the *being* art of Reiki. These exchanges can have a substantive, deep and soothing effect—at many, and upon the multidimensional levels of *being*. Here is a way to make a beginning toward opening our "inner vision," and to evoke a renewed zest for life.

See "Suggested Reading" Appendix C

2. Interconnectedness

*O*ver the years, I have come to see how each person with whom I have interacted in my ongoing practice of Reiki is, for me, a unique portal to all humanity. Each of us is an expression of the Whole of Humanity, and contains the Whole. That which **is** comes from an Order in which everything is folded into everything, and, in the most fundamental sense, each of us is interconnected with the Whole, and to all others.

"You don't stop at your skin."

Dolores Krieger, Ph.D., R.N.

*J*n the past half century, astrophysical, quantum mechanical, astronomical and biological theorists, among others have been exploring the concept of *interconnectedness*. In the healing arts this subject has come to the fore, as well. Dolores Krieger, Ph.D., R.N. and creative force behind Therapeutic Touch with whom I conversed recently, puts it plainly: *"You don't stop at your skin!"*

A broader, bolder vision of life is emerging—one which includes our dual citizenship in both a physical and energetic realms. Within this model, our interconnectedness in a vast sea of life cannot be denied. The following story, shared by a former teacher and current Reiki Master of *The Usui System of Reiki*, which takes place just outside a Fourth Grade classroom in the Deep South, illustrates this point. It involves a science experiment inspired by the research of Marcel Vogel.

Vogel, you may recall, was the brilliant, award-winning IBM research scientist whose findings in the field of liquid crystals (whereby he concluded that **intent** manifests some type of energy field), inspired him to examine the effects of human thought and emotion on plants. Vogel affixed electrodes to his pet philodendron, then hooked it up to a galvanometer (lie-detector). The scientist would breathe deeply, relax, stand close to his philodendron and then let flow showers of affectionate intentions upon the plant as he held his hands, outstretched,

"We are the living links in a life-force that moves and plays through and around us, binding the deepest osils with the farthest stars."

Alan Chadwick

towards it. As if on cue, the plant would respond with a series of ascending oscillations and corresponding leaf movements which, in repeated tests, would register on the galvanometer's recording chart!

The aforementioned Fourth Grade class read about Vogel's work in their *Weekly Reader*. They were intrigued with the notion of interconnectedness. Deciding to prove to themselves the merits of this theory, each adopted a plant. Along the length of their portable classroom (a lightly constructed architectural afterthought more conducive to "open education" than its drab appearance implied) they dug a narrow plot. About mid-February, after lovingly and painstakingly planting a variety of botanical treasures, they began to observe and to "relate to" their plants, affectionately.

Across the way, in another portable, the Fifth Grade teacher, seemed to be forever feeding live rodents to that class' boa constrictor, but, the Fourth-graders were more interested in experimenting in "creative", as opposed to "consumer" research. They wanted to "communicate" with their plants on an "energy" level. Some of the older students, already firmly enmeshed in the restrictive confines of a purely polar worldview, joked about this, but the "Fourth-graders," having the benefit of documented research, were sophisticated! They brushed aside disbelief and scoffing with the wise words, "Just wait and see!"

By May, all the plants were thriving, but two students began to have spectacular experiences. Pedro, admired for his "good-eye" (focused eye) in baseball, and a green thumb he attributed to working the fields before and after school, and poetic Beth, of the tender, blue eyes, and quiet, gentle ways, who looked at her plant the way a new mother regards her baby, grew plants that were measurably larger than the others, and *moved* as the children stroked them *from a good distance*. Everyone noticed!

By early June, a ritual of "live observation" had evolved. The whole class would line up on the inside of the portable to peer out the generous windows. Beth and Pedro, on the outside and in full view of the Fifth and Sixth-graders, began their demonstration. They would smile at their plants as if they were their favorite schoolyard buddies, admire them and touch them gently. Next, stepping back a few inches they would begin to move their hands, repeatedly, from top to bottom of the plant, down-down-and-down again; until the *leaves actually began to wave*, and a whole group of nine, ten, and eleven year old kids, not to mention a couple of amazed teachers, knew that they had encountered a force unseen. Vogel, who in his Palo Alto lab, had concluded that *an invisible life-force envelopes living creatures, making possible "a mutual sensitivity allowing [us] not only to intercommunicate, but to record the communications,"* had nothing on these Fourth-graders. They understood how the very real power of abundant good wishes expresses itself, and impacts other living creatures... in an interconnected Whole. This was a good lesson learned in the realm of energetics... a good lesson learned in becoming aware of the dynamic interaction between the physical and energetic realms.

Interconnectedness is a dynamic interaction, in a multidimensional arena that is typified by receptivity, reciprocity, and potentiality. It is integral to the art of Reiki, and to an understanding of the challenges before the global community.

Try this:

Go to the garden shop or greenhouse of your choice. With the material you have just read in mind, look for a section of plants with which you appear to have an affinity.

Purchase a plant to which you sense you can "relate." Follow the procedure of "magic" used by the Fourth Grade class. Record notes and observations.

What does this tell you about interconnectedness?

Wise Words

Gregory Bateson - *"It takes two to know one."*

David Bohm - *"The individual is universal, and the universal is individual... individuality is only possible if it unfolds from wholeness."*

Pierre Teilhard de Chardin - *(There is a)"fantastic spectacle staring us in the face, of a rapidly rising collective reflection, moving in step with an increasingly unitary organization."*

Ilya Prigogine - *"The idea of simplicity is falling apart...any direction you go in there's complexity."*

Allowing

Presence
Spread your light
Through what is essentially empty.
Become transparent
In our midst
As we, in turn,
Become your conduits.

- Else -

What would the meadowlark
Do in the Spring
Could he not sing of
His fullest vocation —
To be the Window of the Creator —
To be the creation?

- And -

What would the artist
Do in her loft,
If not, soft
In transparent imagery,
Become herself,
Harmonious Consciousness?

Wind-in-the-Feather

3. Openness and "Ki" Catalyst

Some Good Questions

? What is "Ki?"?
? How do we become aware of it?
? How do we connect with it to induce tranquility?
? What is its relationship with Openness?
? What unknown worlds lie beyond those we perceive?

"Finding "Ki" involves an interesting process of learning to cut through illusion, to realize that we are not just physical beings in a physical reality..."

*W*hat unknown worlds lie beyond those we perceive? In realms unaccustomed to dualistic, subject-object, polarized review, celebrated vistas might reveal themselves, as new relationships arise, in a super-sensing world! "*Ki*" and its associate, *Openness* are energetic portals to what lies beyond our ken. These elements are interrelated, yet are as distinct as sound waves and heat waves, candlelight and firelight. What is "*Ki*?" How do we become aware of it? Then, how do we connect with it to induce tranquility? - and perhaps celebrate an awakening? Good questions. The following checklist will show you how many answers you already have!

What you Already Know May Surprise You

Have you ever walked into a business meeting late, and, in the silence, "felt" the air charged with "electricity?"

☐ Yes   ☐ No

Check the appropriate box.

Have you ever "*felt*" someone walking behind you, even though you could not see the person, or "*felt*" drained or exhilarated around another?

☐ Yes   ☐ No

Have you ever squinted at the area surrounding the plants in a summer garden, just after it rains, and "imagined" you saw a mirage-like, transparent energy there?

☐ Yes   ☐ No

Has your whole body kind of gotten "jumpy" during a thunderstorm?

☐ Yes   ☐ No

Has someone walked into a crowded room and headed straight toward you even though s/he'd never met you, or had any idea of who you were?

☐ Yes   ☐ No

Can you tell how someone's feeling just by the "atmosphere" around him or her, even though they may tell you that they are feeling differently than what you think?

☐ Yes   ☐ No

Have you ever been day-dreaming about your favorite person in the world, and suddenly felt a surge in energy?

☐ Yes   ☐ No

Has your hair ever "stood-on-end" when someone walked by you? Have you ever liked or disliked someone on first sight?

☐ Yes   ☐ No

If you have a total of three or more yes answers, you "know" about "Ki", and if you, like most people, answered "yes" to some, or all, of these questions, you have already experienced "*Ki*", and through it, your connection with the cosmos.

4. "Ki"

"Ki" is defined as that alive energy that permeates all living things.

Awareness of *"Ki"* can be vague at first, but increases with recognition of it in everyday encounters, such as those in the previous checklist. Practicing Reiki is a good way to increase this awareness. We are alive with *"Ki."* It is always present and available. Plants have it. Kids in the school yard have it. "Couch potatoes" have it. Lovers, snuggling, have it. Poets and programmers have it. You have it. I have it. All living creatures *have* it. The question is not if we have it, but is... how do we become consciously aware of "Ki?" One answer is to allow ourselves the chance to engage this energetic phenomenon through practing contemplation and Reiki.

Recognizing "Ki"

Recognizing "Ki" is a natural result of the increased awareness of a living cosmos garnered in the art of the practice of Reiki. The more you allow yourself to sink in to the stillness of the Reiki moment, the more sensitive you become to your own energy vacillations, and to those of others. It is easy to do, and we will explore this later on in the book. In the meantime, investiage the experiment in the margin.

Finding "Ki"

Some people see *"Ki"* in halos and auras, but most people do not. That is not because they cannot, or because it does not exist. It is just because they are untrained.

Finding "Ki" can be fun and interesting. If you do not trust what you cannot see, you might try something more technologically sophisticated than your own crude physical instruments (eyes, ears, etc.). Look up the data from Stanford University, Material Sciences

> **Try this:**
>
> *Sit in your office or personal space at home. Cover your eyes. Ask a friend to enter the room silently. Can you feel when this happens? If so, you are tuning-in to someone else's energy...tuning-in to "Ki". How does the awareness of "Ki" strike You?*

*"Prana [Ki] is the expression
of manifesting Being."*

Maharishi Mahesh Yogi

Facilities. Some time ago, Dr. William A. Tiller put together a team of researchers, equipped with ultra-sensitive electromagnetic measuring devices who documented that "*Ki*" extends beyond the surface of living things. In the human being, it brightens the area around the body (you do *to* have an aura!) especially the head (you do have a halo!).

Tiller and his researchers dubbed the energy field in the area close to the body the human energy field (HEF). The HEF has been the subject of on-going research and analysis in hospitals and other research centers as well. Here experiments indicate its life-affirming aspects, and its role in accelerating healing.

Finding "*Ki*" involves an interesting process of learning to cut through illusion. We can then come to realize that we are not just physical beings in a physical reality. We are also vibrant, vibrating energy systems.

The practice of Reiki can help us to relax into feeling comfortable as we assimilate the information, which hundreds of years and hundreds of thousands of scientists in conscientious enterprise have produced. To **experience** multidimensional perception in a fabric of **being** that is close to, as well as beyond, our bodies–is a possibility for all Reiki practitioners!

Reiki is simple, yet cosmic. It is available, open to, surging through/with*in* all living creatures—and with*out*—in the spaces between us—that indeed *unite* us! We, as vibrating fields of energy, are as *in* the cosmos, as the cosmos is *in* us. Thus, we approach the result of millions of years of evolutionary unfolding to discover that, the Reiki practice opens the way to a *new way of seeing* our own nature where we are unencumbered by our sense of separateness as we celebrate a release into a very hospitable domain!

*"We are not just physical beings in a physical reality.
We are much more."*

Light of the Inner Garden

Look at the butterfly
Tumbling from cocoon
Easing into a renaissance
Of color, and of light; swooning;
Freeing essence
From the night.

O Being of profound integration,
O hallowed one, O celebration,
Tranquility;
Integrity, drifting into flight,
You are the silent flutter
Of profound insight.

Wind-in-the-Feather

New Images

Contemporary scientific research confirms the existence of subtle energy fields encompassing living creatures. In the human being, these are known as "subtle bodies." They can be detected by scientific instruments as they "vibrate" beyond our physical extremities. Ancient texts referred to these as layers of extending energy. This is not romanticism, or wishful thinking. This is **real**.

Adjusting to the fact that scientists worldwide, have demonstrated that we can perceive energy extending beyond all living creatures. We can: 1) delineate the subtle bodies just beyond our physical ones and we can, 2) become familiar with these energy bodies and their patterns of moving energy... can be challenging for a populace raised on baseball, apple pie, a solid work ethic and the good old dependable Newtonian model of reality. Still, every day, scientific research is corroborated. Many, many reputable individuals, such as Norm, have moved beyond the "apparent" to come face to face with this emerging understanding—much as once we moved beyond the notion that the world is flat.

Indeed, some people have even learned to recognize certain energy patterns as having particular significance (such as Norm did in his statement - "What makes a place special is the *energy*."). There are also energy patterns relative to growth, healing, and general well-being. Pioneers of a new way of seeing are discovering these. One such person, a medical doctor who "reads" auras, is Robert T. Jaffe, M.D. As a medical doctor, Jaffe operates within specified legal constraints. Dr. Jaffe must substantiate diagnoses he makes as a result of his perceptions of the subtle bodies. He insists upon documentation of his observations with laboratory analysis. Results confirm his diagnoses.

Jaffe, not only practices allopathic and wholistic medicine, but also teaches doctors, nurses, and others interested in subtle energy *how* to perceive it. He maintains that such "vision" is not difficult to

"Our task must be to free ourselves... by widening our circle of compassion to embrace all living beings and all of nature."

Albert Einstein

achieve once one is attuned to it. He says that if there is a problem that resides in the mind-body, it can influence one's whole being, causing "a twisting, or contraction of the energy field."

Before this twisted energy moves into the physical body, you can release it energetically through a combination of Reiki, contemplative relaxation, an understanding of what the root causal factors are, and knowledge of how energy flows. Expanding on that thought for a moment, we see how the possibility opens up to reveal how we are *participants with* rather than *controllers of* the process of Wellness or Wholeness... a significant benchmark in our unfolding process.

Listen to this, and hear the mystery inside.."

Rumi

Human beings are dynamic energy systems interconnected in an organic way to all living creatures and to Earth Mother. As we know, the world is not static. It is dynamic. If we replace reductionist... purely physical reality... thinking with synthesis/systems thinking we can develop new relationships within ourselves and among living communities. Through earnest enterprise, we can dissolve unhealthy restrictive energy patterns. We can see our way to a new commitment, and with it a new hope, for ourselves and for the global community. By arranging pictures in our minds of Wholeness (Wellness) in the world-at-large, by telling "my" story that touches everyone and all creatures around me in an integral, natural community reflective of the fully functioning me, I participate as a catalyst for change in the new story. This is the larger meaning of energy flow in the big picture.

Before developing new inner/outer vision, however, we need to have an *awareness*... we need to "see" energy. Today's technology can and does aid us. In fact, scientists have established "maps" of the pathways of flowing energy, and documented this in their laboratories. Indeed, they have demonstrated that energy flow has direction, and that the flow is visible and registers (even sometimes to the human eye).

So what is seen?

Energy Patterns and Pathways

*E*nergy patterns and pathways are observable - "Ki", life-force energy, moves from head downward, through trunk, arms, hands, legs and feet, along meridians in the body, through a series of "chakras"—energy centers. It concentrates around living things, as a field of energy; in human beings, the HEF. It also extends out in space as an overall life-force field! The implications of this **fact** are far-reaching.

"*Ki*" flows in, out, about, and through living creatures, freely, and in a balanced way—when you are feeling relaxed and well. However, if you are feeling puny, distressed, or very ill, the flow of *"Ki"* is blocked, scattered or diminished.

You don't have to be a genious to figure out that just recognizing "*Ki*" is not enough. We need to know how to open, or to attune to its restorative effects. Then we can interact with, or draw, "*Ki.*" One of my teachers advised me to think of it as committing to good banking practices. "Fiscal exchanges of an energy sort," one might say. "But first," he admonished, "you must open the account!"

"The irresistible Vortex ... spins into itself always in the same direction...the whole Stuff of Things, from the most simple to the most complex; spinning into ever more comprehensive and astronomically complicated nuclei...and the result of this structural portion is an increase in consciousness."

Pierre Teilhard de Chardin

5. Openness

Openness is an energetic key. When it is practiced in Reiki, it has the quality of holding a "space" for something much like opening a bank account does. You are creating a "space" in which you can transact exchanges and funnel them. *Openness*, then can be seen as *opportunity*. With the slightest mental adjustment, just a bit of imagery, it is possible to "open the account" and utilize this agent of change.

Energy Exchange

The empty channel you have observed in your bathtub is a metaphor for *Openness* described in the Reiki practice. *Openness* allows for the transference of "Ki". This is a life-affirming transaction/exchange. *Openness* potentiates the opportunity to access inner vision and inner wisdom. *Openness* supports a give-and-take, so that one is available both to share "Ki," and to draw upon "Ki." *Openness, as* **experienced** *in the practice of Reiki, potentiates abundance, change, nurturance, and accelerates healing on a personal and global level.*

After you have seen a whirlpool (or vortex) and the open channel within it in the "comfort of your own home" so to speak, it is easy to imagine, is it not? What you might not know is that the process is also quite simple and simply delightful.

See if visualizing "Ki" being *drawn* through the open place within that swirling mass of energy is something you can do.

Try this:

After you read this page, please put down this book, and draw a nice, aromatic, relaxing bath.

Get in.

After you have enjoyed it, open the drain all the way, and closely observe the swirling vortex at that drain (a whirlpool in your bathtub).

Note that in the center, within this spiraling mass, just as within the eye of a hurricane, there is an empty channel. This space of **emptiness** *is possibility... it can represent the open channel, the conduit, accessed in the practice of Reiki.*

Drawing "Ki" from the Bank

It is easy to draw energy from the "Bank of Ki" in the Reiki *experience*. The act of deciding to *draw* it... conscious intention... creates the possibility, or *Openness*. This is the "secret" necessary for the transmission of vital energy. In other words, when you decide to take good care of you, as a unique, connected member of our living cosmos, you carve a space within yourself that is ready to accept abundant blessings. You are in a "being" artform in which all "beingness" is available for you – and through You to the organic whole.

When we come to a comprehensive awareness of the interdependence of all life on our planet–when we come to see Mother Earth as what she is–a living, organic, unfolding phenomenon–and when we see ourselves not just as observers, but as participants in a wondrous evolutionary unfolding–then the "Bank of 'Ki'" holds the promise of mutual development and revivification.

Motto: Be a Verb.

Try this:

Use your imagination. Visualize a vortex. Then pretend you are a whirlpool of human energy, with a golden cylinder (funnel) which starts near your halo, above the top of your head.

Get a clear image of this in your mind's eye.

What do you make of the picture? Get comfortable with it. Make sure it is now very clear in your mind's eye.

Now visualize "Ki" (like Pixie glitter) swishing into your channel from the energetic spaces just beyond your body.

Visualize yourself drinking in (drawing) revitalizing energy through the crown of your head, and through every system of your body. (You can also try this with the subtle body if you can imagine it.)

Next, imagine sharing this energy in a living bio system with others, and the Planet's global community.

"One of the most pernicious illusions developed in the heart of man during the course of history is the pseudo-evidence of his completeness and fixity."

Pierre Teilhard de Chardin

Taking Good Care of You

- Sit quietly.
- Breathe deeply. (See Breathing technique, Appendix B.) Inhale. Release with compassion all that is heavy and distressing. Exhale.
- Center yourself in an open nonlocal space; and continue conscious breathing.
- Note that you are consciously breathing in difficulties, releasing them to breath out freshness for all living creatures.
- Fold your hands over your heart.
- Now, envision a peaceful, safe place in which you are secure and can rest.
- Pretend you are a living vessel, a fantabulous, enormous redwood tree just waiting to drink in the elixir of life.
- Keep breathing, consciously. Keep hands folded over heart.
- Focus your attention by holding the image you have created of the tranquil place and the "open" awaiting receptacle.
- RELAX, and OPEN to possibility; feel "*Ki*" flowing, naturally, being drawn like the warmth of sunlight to every part of you—easing tension, replenishing deficits, melting away obstructions—leaving you relaxed, renewed, refreshed—and able to share new vigor with the human community and with the world-at-large. CELEBRATE.

> *Use the following step-by-step formula.*
> *Note before and after sensations.*

*N*otice, you are <u>not</u> trying to get certain results. You are simply making yourself available (OPEN) to "being" energized. You are, therefore, consciously allowing. Reiki is a ***being*** artform. You have reached a special state, called passive volition that says: "Never mind hanging on to your personal (ego) defenses...Never mind results!...Just **BE, Now!**"

*Y*ou have now completed a dance called *"just being and relaxing."* What is your inner voice saying? What do you feel? You have put yourself in the position of being able to recognize the nonlocal, nonphysical quality of *Openness*. You now hold an understanding of an important key to profound relaxation... and to a bold new view of yourself as a physical and energetic citizen of the Cosmos.

Would you like to access this "space" of *Openness* as you feel the need? If you learn to recognize "Alpha," it's a snap!

Viewing Life, A Code

Lie on your back
'neath the trees in the Spring.

Let your nose be your guide
whilst faeries Sing.

Slide your eyes down the tip
to the leaves at the Top.

Daydream, on the ground,
of Life without stop!

See, in the sky,
a stream passing by.

Join it there, with your Heart;
in Mid-air.

Wind-in-the-Feather

6. "Alpha" and Alpha!

*D*id you know that we can train our brains to produce the electrical output most conducive to passive volition? The training is called "alpha biofeedback" from the brain wave pattern induced, and from the method of induction. Since the "alpha" state is particularly conducive to suspending tension and appears to offer an alternative to years of practice in various forms of meditation (which also produces the desired state) it has become quite popular. How did this come about, and how does it relate to the next "Ki"-Key?

"Each small task of everyday life is part of the total harmony of the universe."

St. Theresa of Lisieux

*I*n the early 1940's, when biofeedback was in its infancy, researchers discovered that the brain wave activity of their subjects fell in step with the same pattern of light emission as was seen in flickering firelight. They were able to measure the electrical output of the brain in the resulting relaxed, but alert, state. It was characterized by an EEG pattern showing bursts of alpha (8 to 13hz) and frequencies ranging in amplitude from 150uv or more...*the same as those measured in meditators.*

You may have never imagined that Yogis, meditating in exotic temples, and Scouts, telling tales by campfire, had much in common, yet research proves otherwise. Findings indicate that these two very diverse groups, in approaching a relaxed but alert state, both produce higher levels of serotonin, and beta endorphin neuro-chemicals, and experience significant muscular relaxation. More interesting, perhaps, is the discovery that once you are aware of the "alpha state," you can reproduce it at will. Like riding a bike, once you know how, *you know how*! Achieving this state is readily available through the practice of Reiki.

Somewhere between biofeedback, scouting, and years of consistent practice in meditation, in nonlocal space, requiring only your committed willingness and attention, lies the practice of Reiki. Here, many Reiki participants, and most experienced practitioners, produce "alpha" automatically, and easily identify and use it. If there is a "how to" in the Reiki *experience*, it's "how to" reach this state.

Recognizing and Accessing Alpha

*R*ecognizing, and being able to move to "Alpha" and Alpha!, is an important factor in practicing Reiki for Relaxation. Here are two experiments. One takes 21 days. The other can be immediate.

Try this:

*If you want to find the "alpha" frequency, take a **Reiki Break**, twice a day, for at least fifteen minutes, at dawn and dusk, for three weeks.*

Within 21 days, You should recognize a shift as you move into a relaxed, alert mode.

"I've learned more from watching my dogs than from all the great books I've read!."

Gerry Spence
Illustrious Storyteller and Attorney

Just *BE*, Right Now

- Stay present.
- Take a relaxing, deep, deep breath…and just let go…
- In and out—breathing, now—**notice** your breathing.
- Now, pretend you are playing baseball and it is your turn up to bat, and you have got your eye on the ball (*"good eye"*).
- Stay with the sense of the moment for so long as you can—and keep breathing.
- Balance yourself between being relaxed and being alert, and keep focused for a minute, or two, or five, or—here's Alpha!*

If you are a keen, competent, and confident observer of **NOW**, you will surely recognize "Alpha" and Alpha! However, just **BEING**, or just *doing nothing at all*, in your Reiki session may lead you to the alert, but relaxed state and "Alpha!" which is a by-product of the Reiki practice. No effort required! It just *happens*, as part of the artform.

Centered

At the Crossroads of Here and Now,
At that Moment
Lies Potentiality
And a Choice of
Whether to be alert to the Moment,
Or to risk losing contact with Self
In veiled moments
Extending on, and on
Into a Lifetime
Of Illusion.

Wind-in-the-Feather

7. Integrity and Core Harmony

*T*o choose, in stillness at "the crossroads" as the preceding poem suggests, means to become aware of the inner tensions arising from spanning time; from past to future. We become conscious when we pause *to BE* in the *Now*.

Deep within is knowledge of the richness of the new, which yearns for recognition. By being mindful in the moment the Witness Self participates in the Reiki *experience*. This is "anchored" in the *Now*. Through Reiki, we can perceive our internal space with clarity, access inner wisdom, as well as moderate our external "space." We can facilitate accepting ourselves. Reiki helps us to draw upon the full extent of our **being**. The practice can release the knotted up tension of concealed injury, the pain of the past, the unprocessed experience, and can lessen insecurity borne of an unknown future.

In her books and workshops, psychologist and Usui Reiki Master Paula Horan, Ph.D. deals extensively with the "Core Self, the very heart of your Being." She addresses the real, limitless you. "It is totally uplifting [to] experience your true identity and potential," she says, and goes on to point out that Reiki (the *experience* and vital energy) "will eventually guide you to the experience that you, yourself, **are** Reiki, or Universal Life-force Energy."

"Well, let's see…"

Norm

*B*eing centered, in your business life or in your personal life, starts with self inquiry… an inner vision of You, within and without, in relationship to the Whole. You have heard the words, "To thine own self be true." Have you ever wondered just who **You** are, the "True **You**?" You may not explore these questions frequently, yet until you know *who you are* and then relax into accepting, and being yourself, how can you relate to yourself, or to others, freely and wholeheartedly?

I am reminded of the Tibetan chant, *"Om mani padme hum"*

Over the years, I've come to see that *Integrity and Core Harmony* in synergistic relationship with *Potentiality* are counterparts, in an emphatic trajectory. Reiki practice structures the possibility for recognizing and feeling synchronized with True Self. In the Reiki *experience* you support your ability to handle difficult situations, to resolve sticky issues or relationships, to release stress, and to enjoy inner peace, thereby contributing to global harmony.

Reiki participation and practice facilitates opening to and celebrating life, while you are just **being** where you are, when you are there.

8. Attending <u>Now,</u> and Being

*T*he enterprise or discovering and honoring your core self requires focus. Focus is the ability to pay attention, in a present moment, to **being** where you are.

If you intend, through the practice of Reiki, to potentiate well-being (for example, to balance relaxation, stress and anxiety) and so become more aware of energetic transactions… you will need to be able to quiet persistent rumblings of your "logical" mind… to focus upon the here and now. Thus, the Reiki practice centers around *Attending - Now and Being*. Put simply, the Reiki experience can enable you to summon up a point of stillness through visualization and imagining.

Where can you go in your mind's eye to seek focus? If you see empty spaces as possibilities, where in your imagination, do you feel grounded in groundlessness, and centered in an ocean of pure potentiality? Find it, and all possibility opens to you. Set aside this book and begin the journey by discovering what works for you.

*A*ttending Now and Being is a process. A fellow Reiki practitioner, Barbara Marrett, in her book, <u>Mahina Tiare!</u>, recounting the story of her sailing adventure from Friday Harbor (Washington State) to the South Seas declares, "We were steering by hand, and it was all I could manage to keep the boat on course." Here is a metaphor for the process of attending.

Course correction, whether accomplished in a boat at sea on an "inner journey" can be challenging. It requires attention. The ability to attend to the moment at hand is a mark of the energetically-aware person. This capacity grows with practice and requires focus, ("steering by hand") which ensures that we reach our destination. In the case of

---

Try this:

Imagine, or go to a summer meadow that's just throbbing with scent, sound, color, attractive spaces, shafts of luminous splendid, mystery…

Imagine that you are gently swaying in a "Magic Hammock" (as referenced in Chapter One).

Relax, and focus your attention on your breathing. Bravely breathe in all distress. Notice it. Notice if as a phenomenon common to all living creatures, and compassionately release it. Now, Slowly exhale. Watch your breath and your breathing until you are totally aware of it.

Now place your hands on your knee and focus your attention on it.

This evokes a conscious experience of Now awareness in which your physical body grounds your attention.

See how this experience combines both physicality and energetics and is aligned with your true nature.

the practice of Reiki, we create an opening for celebrating live, which fosters a vigilant attitude by grounding us in the physical task at hand.

*H*ow much of your experience in life takes place in the ***Now*** moment? How much takes place in your fearful imagination?—or wishful thinking? (For example - when you are brushing your teeth in the morning, are you really someplace else? or, are you saying to yourself, "Wow, I'm brushing my teeth, and I hope all teeth in the world are feeling as good as mine?") How much of your life is a reaction, a return to the past, or a fantasy?

Use the following "Check-in" to review your present moment staying power.

"It is in giving oneself that one receives it; it is in forgetting oneself that one is found; it is in pardoning that one obtains pardon."

St. Francis of Assisi

Whenever we pray, we always pray 'mitakuye oyasin', for all our relations. We pray for all of the black people, all of the yellow people, all the white people, and all the red people. We pray for all our relations.

Lakota Elder

Present Moment Staying Power

	Yes	No
Opened my eyes in the morning?	☐	☐
Bathed?	☐	☐
Brushed teeth?	☐	☐
Exercised?	☐	☐
Got dressed?	☐	☐
Kissed someone?	☐	☐
Had morning meal?	☐	☐
Started day's activities?	☐	☐
Cared for others?	☐	☐
Talked with first person?	☐	☐
Handled business over the phone?	☐	☐
Went through the day, (by the hour?)	☐	☐
Talked with last person?	☐	☐
Hugged someone?	☐	☐
Settled in at home?	☐	☐
Watered the plants?	☐	☐
Petted the cat, played with the dog.	☐	☐
Listened to music?	☐	☐
Practiced Reiki?	☐	☐
Fixed dinner?	☐	☐
Snuggled?	☐	☐

How's your present moment staying power?
Check the boxes, and note.

Try this for 21 days. Evaluate the percentages. What percentage of your present moments are reactive. What percentage are absent? What percentage are **Now**?

* Hint: Practice Reiki upon opening eyes in morning. See what happens.

Unfolding NOW

Doing is familiar. But *allowing* right now, or releasing the mind's distractions, *observing* is an artform. You may find that when you are the observer of all that is going on in your life , you don't get trapped into reacting to memories. Neither do you have expectations of the future. You are just here, ***Now***. And in this happy space, you change.

You might view attempting to let go by being mindful, (focused), as challenging. I have come to see that it can be accessible within the context of the practice of Reiki. Here, the "Ki"-Keys of *Attending Now and Being* crystallize the interaction of inner truth with that of the cosmic whole. When one lives life at each moment, an organic dynamic unfolds... a shift towards the positive, along with dissolved stress, and a sense of well-being in relationship to the entire synergistic system.

Again, I quote Dr. Paula Horan. From the course of years of Reiki practice, she says, "We tend to lose our addiction to intellectual explanations. Instead, we begin to live in the moment. We experience life at a gut level, with our immediate and spontaneous feelings [rather than] in our heads - with thoughts that divide and separate."

Mindfulness, (*Attending Now and Being*), means that you can recognize yourself as separate from your thoughts. You can untether yourself from projecting those thoughts upon yourself and others. By practicing, or by participating in Reiki, you are exercising your capacity to deliberately alter your stance in relationship to life situations. You do this not by shutting yourself off from the situations or by subjecting yourself to them; but by accepting; embracing **what is** and with full attention, sinking into the pain, and into the emptiness— or the pleasure and bliss—trusting the birth of the new. With this perception, you look at life's process and say, "What can I learn from this?" Thus, you create the path of your life, and carve out a space in which your unique agendae are seen for what they are, within the full range of your highest consciousness and within the full spectrum of *possibility*!

Catalysts

*P*articipating in the Reiki process encourages not only relaxation, but the activation of certain energetic skills that you already have, of which you might yet be unaware. These capacities are *agents of change*. The "Ki"-Keys potentiate expanded awareness.

We come to see that the practice of Reiki is about learning receptivity by trusting ourselves in openness, stillness, empathy, attunement to energy and pure potential. We do this as dual citizens of physical and energetic realms. Indeed, we can sculpt spaces... spaces of possibility... spaces full of surprise and delight... spaces bolder than any previously imagined. And, in these "Reiki spaces," we can experience ourselves, others and our universe compassionately, because through the practice of Reiki, we become like hollow channels through which Life Energy resonates.

As a methodology, Reiki is pro-active, it is a creative artform much like a duet played ensemble by practitioner and recipient, (or by practitioner and a state of relaxed optimal well-being). It *can* be a "fugue" of melodic proportion involving practitioner/recipient, cosmos, and Cosmos. Your *experience* with Reiki depends upon your willingness to enter into the "moment", into a new way of being.

Experience has shown that in becoming fluent in the many facets, and in the artful practice of "energy medicine", you fund inner strength. This you can rely upon. Moreover, this juicy practice opens the possibility for renewed creativity, for a transformation of consciousness. As you continue to explore, to accept, and to empower yourself, you will notice that you are able to "see" energetically as well as physically... you can now come to a mode of being that starts from the encompassing Whole, and then touches others (sub-wholes) in a dynamic, interconnected, wholistic world beyond. You can begin with practical explorations in the very next chapter.

| **Check-in Summary** |

		Yes	No	Maybe
1.	You have an energy field (HEF).	☐	☐	☐
2.	Your soft boundaries are measurable by modern state-of-the-art scientific instrumentation.	☐	☐	☐
3.	Your boundaries are *not* your physical extremities.	☐	☐	☐
4.	When you are relaxed, energy flows easily through your energy field.	☐	☐	☐
5.	You are capable of recognizing your own life-force energy, and that of other living creatures.	☐	☐	☐
6.	You can refine your skills, and expand your awareness to see the world in a new way; that is, ***energetically***.	☐	☐	☐
7.	Through Reiki can facilitate change, and an unfolding to a higher order of consciousness.	☐	☐	☐
8.	You are able to empathize.	☐	☐	☐
9.	You are able at times to "stay present" in the present.	☐	☐	☐
10.	You are striving for "core" harmony.	☐	☐	☐

If you check yes on four or more below, you're on the road to understanding energy medicine.

"Supposing… we now try, if only by some trick of the mind, to shift our outlook unreservedly into that of a world which is evolving?…."

Pierre Teilhard de Chardin

The Reiki Methodology
A Participatory Model

Anthem

We living creatures
We felicitous fields
of patterns
of energy
of Life-force Energy
Boundless Ki, of a Limitless Source;
interconnected
resonating, living creatures
flowing with potential's course;
Now one with the Whole,
as whirlpools in a Stream,
Now distinct within the Whole,
as whirlpools in a Stream,
Open to receive,
free to align
with design
mystical,
Reflections of the
Organizing Principle,
ever present
ever magical
We living creatures
Are the fugues of
resonant being.

Wind-in-the-Feather

"If you help others, you will be helped, perhaps tomorrow, perhaps in one hundred years, but you will be helped. Nature must pay off the debt... It is a mathematical law and all life is mathematics."

Gurdjieff

Innate Capacities

*L*et's suppose that, like Usui, you have a burning desire. Let's suppose that your heartfelt wish is to retain your equilibrium in the midst of all the goings-on in your life, to release the need to control, to move into a participatory mindset, and glean the resulting health benefits—maybe even come to a deeper awareness of the Universe. Let's then suppose that in order to meet your needs, you decide actively to practice Reiki. What can you expect?

The first thing you can expect is that you will find yourself more "in the flow," doing so many things "right," that you won't be able to count them! Attuned to Reiki to *Life-force Energy*, which abides in an interconnected, interrelated, dynamic Whole, you facilitate moving into stillness, and in that moment, balancing energy. Thus, you are your best ally in accelerating the healing process! *The Usui System of Reiki* simply focuses attention on an innate capacity.

Attuning

*P*racticing Reiki interjects energy on many levels. You have the potential to reinterpret events in your life. You can evaluate the significance those events hold for you. You can reorganize yourself in a positive direction—because you are the artist creating the masterpiece.

I made a list the other day of all the methods of just "letting-go" in the moment that I could call to mind… from A to Z… there were "attitude adjustment," biking, cantering through the mountain valleys just after sunrise, dancing, etc.… all the way to yoga, and Zen cooking. These are all things you *do* or *learn to do* to reorient yourself in timespace. They all work, but Reiki, a being artform, is *different*. Here's how: Lineage and Ceremony. Let me explain.

Being Different

*R*eiki itself, not the methodology, but Universal Life-force Energy, is all encompassing. Here's how Rick Bockner, one of just twenty-two Reiki Masters hand-trained by Takata during her four decades of teaching explains it: "Reiki is to us like the ocean is to the creatures who live in it - the medium in which they abide." Rick is alluding to the fact that we are "energetic beings" who thrive in a vibrant, resonating field of energy while drawing through ourselves life-force energy ("Ki"). Reiki "itself" is alive energy.

Reiki, the *methodology*, is a hands-on practice which serves to catalyze Reiki *Universal Life-force Energy*. Reiki, the methodology, distinguishes itself also as "energy medicine". In addition, Reiki is different from other "releasing" or "awareness expanding" methodologies in the following ways: lineage and ceremony.

Lineage

*T*he Reiki methodology is supported by an unbroken lineage of hand-trained teachers, called Reiki Masters who trace their roots from Takata , to Hayashi , to Dr. Mikao Usui, himself. These teachers of *The Usui System of Reiki* follow a universal process of format and form. A student learning Reiki in Holland, or in India, or in Canada, or in the U.S., is aware that "reikicousins" across the globe follow standard practice. Reiki is taught in the oral tradition by teachers who have promised to explore deeper relationships with life. Like Usui, they try to live as adventurers, as vibrant, integral microcosms contributing to "the bigger picture,"… a cosmic Whole. Like their predecessors, Reiki Masters of *The Usui School of Reiki* are carefully mentored, and are well-versed in helping interested students align with Reiki *Universal Life-force Energy* through the Ceremony of Attunement.

The Ceremony of Attunement

*T*he art of cherishing the eternal *Now*- in which we leap beyond illusory and limiting constraints, requires that we remain alert, still and accepting. Our original nature is all that we are and, without being it, it is also awareness, itself playing in a web of interconnected processes.

In the Ceremony of Attunement, we celebrate a shift of emphasis – as expressed in the Reiki practice from objects (mechanistic model) to events (energetic model). We celebrate an awakening of inner wisdom which understands the dynamic character of reality, and gives rise to a strong sense of the wholistic nature of experience. This in turn leads us to view a dynamic interplay between actuality and possibility, as we come to see our place in a coherent process within a total system.

Mastery expresses itself in *The Ceremony of Attunement*. What *happens* during the ceremony has sometimes been compared with the first time someone flips the switch to light a building already wired. The Reiki Master "flips the switch," and you are "connected," consciously, with the Limitless Whole, the source of "Ki," in *a new way*. This is not to say that you were not "connected" before. Rather that your commitment, in combination with the *Ceremony* , amplifies and accelerates your awareness of Life-force Energy and your "plug-in" points!

In this ceremony, the purpose of which is to communicate directly from one consciousness to the other in order to manifest a transformation of consciousness, a change occurs... be it subtle or significant.

It is important to remember that it is because of *your* commitment, that you open to possibilities. It is because of *your* intent that awareness blossoms. It is by *your* reflection that you come to see. Even though a Reiki Master, in the great tradition of *The Usui System of Reiki*, "gives the blessing" and conducts this ceremony, it is *You*—through self-nurturance, and self-cultivation, not an external authority—who evokes the shift.

To be "attuned" to Reiki means to awaken *a new way of seeing*, a new way of living, and to establish a new global consciousness in which a rigid perception is replaced with celebration of life. In this breakthrough the Whole synergistically reveals Itself.

'Grandfather

Sacred One
Teach us love, compassion, honor
That we may heal the earth
And heal each other.'

Ojibwe Prayer

Therapeutic Reiki

Once a person has experienced The Ceremony of Attunement, that individual can expect a stronger connection with *Life-force Energy*, *"Ki."*

When one is in a state of well-being, *"Ki"* flows freely in... throughout... and from... a living creature, in a *balanced* manner. This has a nourishing effect on all the organs of the body, as well as upon the mind, the emotions, and inner-spirit. Attuned Reiki practitioners, focusing intent on supporting a state of well-being, strengthen or reconnect with Life's pulsing, by approaching a calm, focused state of awareness. (Remember Reiki is a "being" practice.) Practitioners often are able to move beyond their immediate ego needs thus activating an open pathway through which vital energy may flow. Now, an initial intent of relaxation, or tension release, may also induce a quickening, or an expanding awareness of patterns of energy. Moving sequentially, from one position to the next, practitioners can *experience* a thrust toward renewal.

Getting Ready for the Session

*F*or those of you who are reading this and are new to Reiki, may just say that the Reiki *experience* can be powerful. That is why it is a good idea to set aside a few moments to prepare for the Reiki Session. This preparation time is not part of the content of *The Usui System's* methodology or format, just advice from many participants/practitioners/recipients who report that "warming-up" exercises, such as those which follow seem to compliment the session.

Mental Preparation

*I*n preparing for a Reiki Session, you will close your eyes, breathe deeply, and imagine a tranquil scene. Stay focused on this image until your mind and emotions are quiet and a sensation of relaxation occurs. Soon, you can feel centered, as your edges soften. The foreground of your awareness is in rhythm with the **Now**. You are in a "listening" mode, able to detect subtle cues. You remind yourself of your role in the upcoming Session. You focus intent on being present, a catalyst, conduit, or channel for/of *Life-force Energy*.

Physical Preparation

*D*irectly preceding the actual Reiki Session, many participants/recipients, tell us that they employ the following techniques to start relaxing. They advise practicing deep breathing (See Appendix B) and focusing intent exercise in a quiet, warm space where you will be undisturbed. It is nice to select music appropriate for relaxation to accompany the Session, and prepare a comfortable, cushioned table and chair(s).

We like to dim the lights to encourage the process…loosen tight clothing…take off shoes or other constricting items and just close our eyes; mentally clear our minds of the hub-bub of the day, or any other distracting thoughts.

Next, we sweep our hands, from the top of the head to the lower body, while doing an inventory/assessment of sensations, making mental notes and alerting the body that something special is about to begin. If you are offering a Session to someone else, you'd ask if there's anything to which you should be directed. (Do this for yourself, too.)

Warm-up feet and ankles by gently holding insoles, and softly manipulating the area (an old trick I learned from Joan Marie). Important: Pour a glass of water. Drink it after the Reiki Session.

"We are, as the aborigines say, just learning how to survive in infinity."

Michael Talbot
<u>The Holographic Universe</u>

The Actual Session

The placement of hands begins. The vibrant energy flows to receptors in the body-mind-spirit, multidimensional space of the Reiki *experience*. A shift occurs, allowing you to see things *in new ways*.

While breathing and focusing, we progress through each position, scanning, relaxing, and presenting to the mind-body a different "sense". Now this will be transferred into the body. It can bring about physiological changes—the release of tension—the increase of energetic flow.

If a person is tense or is experiencing stress-related illness or symptoms, *"Ki"* is out of balance. As the Reiki Session progresses, that person can draw or pull *"Ki"* as needed. We notice that this process varies in speed and intensity. Fast, slow, sporadic or constant, one continues to draw *Energy* until reaching a point of "Enough." The flow stops. The universe is intelligent, and inherently knows exactly what is needed in establishing individual balance, once life-force energy is activated.

Next, spontaneous changes may commence. It may feel as if a whole layer of "stuff" is sloughed-off or drained away, freeing that which lies beneath; until, finally, *balance* is restored, and a sense of inner peace occurs. Indeed, the practice of Reiki can accelerate the healing process. Imbalance, expressed as tension, stress, irritability, illness, pain, and/or discomfort, clears.

The Reiki Session is an opportunity to reorchestrate one's living dynamic. It is very powerful. It is very simple.

Expectations

*R*eiki is not a system that promises spontaneous healing, yet you can *expect* startling therapeutic responses. If something "miraculous" occurs, it is imperative to remember that Reiki (not you) is the miracle-worker. We are ***not*** **doing** something, rather we are simply **being**, or allowing ourselves to connect with Limitless Potential in a special way similar to the way we resonate with the special energy of a certain place. We invite *"Ki"* to flow through us. Both practitioner and recipient are energized in the process, but do not take on, or give to others, either negativity or Wellness. In *The Usui System of Reiki* it is my/our/ your deep, compassionate, empathic intent to be a catalyst for the highest good of all concerned from the stance of empathy, or compassion that nurtures. What may **be**?...we do not know; we simply trust in the Primary Order. From here, our natural abilities to heal, transcend and transform, proceed.

Metaphors

The following charts attempt to describe the qualities of the subtle energy of Reiki that you may feel physically before and after a Reiki session. Poetry lends itself better to this task than does prose. If the primary colors were analogous to body sensations felt in massage, *then tones and hues* might be analogous to sensations felt in a Reiki Session. Nevertheless, I hope that you will find the words, phrases, metaphors or analogies of interest, and search for some of your own. As I have said, "Reiki's energy is <u>very</u> mysterious!" It is very hard to describe in words.

Whatever words you use to describe the sensations in your hands and body as you progress in your Reiki **experience**, know that skill and sensitivity do intensify with practice. In the final analysis, your own inner-knowing far surpasses descriptive phrases. Nuances are in the realm of intuition, and a very personal thing.

In our society, we express ourselves almost exclusively in words. Yet, in Reiki - in Reiki the *artform*, we trust in quietness. Out of that stillness, that allowing, that openness, we give birth to inner vision, inner wisdom, and peace of mind which touches us on all energetic levels…in our physical and nonphysical being.

Words as Anchors for Awareness

These might indicate imbalance, obstruction or depletion.

Drawing	Numb feelings
Pulling	Wavy heat
Prickly hot denseness	Cold, vacuum-like sensations
Smoggy heaviness	Wooly, thick blanket
Stuffy pressure	

Reiki practitioners' feedback regarding sensations felt in their hands during closing sweep.

These might indicate balanced, or revived energy.

Silkiness	Continuous peaceful pulsing
Smooth	Glowing
Unbroken	Glimmery, expansive
Soft	Flowing, even
Warmth	

Reiki practitioners' feedback regarding sensations felt in their hands at beginning of session in treatment of self and others.

The Cosmic Question

*T*here follows a participatory opportunity. Participating, and therefore experiencing, tells more than all the words the pen can write; experience is "knowing." We can come to see that the practice of Reiki *can* ameliorate the damaging effects of all kinds of stress. We *can* find the energetic space to treat the distress and diseases within ourselves (and the toxicity in our world). We *can* register with an inner knowing that our lives, and our destinies, are interwoven with the workings of Nature. We *can* come to see how "cosmic breath" supports our survival as a living global community. Because the practice of Reiki *can* lead us to experience a knowing of a transcendent, unitive state, it is transformative. The Reiki *experience can* manifest the *wholeness* of our nature, in which distressed *parts* are just a matter of relativity. We body-mind-inner-spirit, our global village, our land-and-seas-and-skies, in balance and harmony, *can* resonate together There is only the question: Are we enterprising enough to reorient our thinking, and to learn ways to express ourselves appropriately just one degree beyond the norm?

Participatory Themes and The Reiki Session

8

Beyond

Who seeks the powers of higher wisdom
On our communal cosmic journey?
In our shared, injured, imperfection
In our weakness, it is told,
We find the splendid gifts of healing.

For if the tears did not admit they cannot cry
And if the ears did not admit they cannot sigh
What assistance would unite us?

the fullness we are siphoning
From each other comes the ripening.
Now to Feast.
Cherish the Banquet,
And share.

Wind-in-the-Feather

Focusing Intent Exercises

Theme One: Eyes
**Hands, fingers and thumbs held together are brought
to rest just over, but not touching, the eyes.**

Statement of Intent: (*Example*) It is my intent to gain a new perspective (eyes) on the issue of understanding other people's point of view (eyes) which has created tension in my life.

Method: (*Example*) Put your hands over your eyes. Breathe…get comfortable…and then "*look at*" a <u>successful</u> conversation you had recently, in which you came to understand someone else *in a new way*. *Notice* that you were relaxed in a state of relaxed alertness quiet but focused. "*Look at*" the environment and <u>see</u> again, the <u>eyes</u>, the expressions during the conversation. Focus your intent, which is to bring even more energy ("Ki"), to an <u>inner vision</u> supporting empathy and strong communication.

Your Statement of Intent:

Your Method: (as above, or…)

Recipient's Impressions

"I felt relieved. I had my hands over my eyes. Quickly I found a "safe place," and I was able to look at things more calmly from this place. Tension lifted."

"Colors shot up against darkness…a neon lime green, a brilliant blue, and this inspired a painting."

"My perception of the world changed."

journal

Theme Two: Ears
Hands are gently drawn to sides of head to rest on either ear and cover TMJ area, joint and jaw bone

Statement of Intent: (*Example*) It is my intent to hear again (ears), the merry sounds of playfulness. I want to bring this into conscious inner-hearing for my project group at work and share it with my partner at home.

Method: (*Example*) Placing my hands upon my ears, I "hear" "Ki" speaking to a remembered childhood scene… maybe it is like the sounds of delight as kids play hide-and-seek…or maybe yelps of surprise. My ears are attuned to the quiet, alert moments of stillness and anticipation as we hide from each other. Again, trying not to burst with laughter as it surges. I am hearing the way I did when I was a child.   I remember the exhilaration as it surges. Transfer the experience, the same delight, to the present, and share.

Your Statement of Intent:

Your Method: (as above, or…)

Recipient's Impressions

"When I was a little kid and I was waiting upstairs for Santa to come, I thought I heard a noise downstairs and my whole body 'listened.' It was as if I tuned in my ears to hear a whisper. That's what happened again with this session."

"I have a problem with clenching my teeth. My wife says I grind them loudly in my sleep. I decided to concentrate on this (second) exercise for three weeks, twice a day. I do it in the morning and just before bed. My jaw feels more relaxed, and so does my wife."

journal

Theme Three: Occipital Lobes
Hands move to back of head where they are now placed under it at the base of the skull. Keep thumbs closed into other fingers. Cradle back of head in palms.

Statement of Intent: (*Example*) It is my intent to make an energetic connection with other members of the living global community through seeing in new ways.

Method: (*Example*) Exhaling and inhaling gently and effortlessly, place hands as directed above. Relax into an imaginary cushion of unconditional acceptance within Mother Nature's arms. Rest in this space. Expect a timeless, floating sensation, as your life-force energy merges with that which surrounds you…extending further and further away…even to the distant Stars, or the trees of an ancient forest. Find an image that attracts you. Mentally ask permission to enter the space of another living being or natural scene. Feel the special energy of that moment, place, or natural wonder. Note that Nature vibrates with life-force energy, of which you are a part.

Your Statement of Intent:

Your Method: (as above, or…)

Recipient's Impressions

"I have never felt more supported in my life! The meaning of 'for the highest good of all concerned' took on new depth."

"I had a throbbing headache when we started the session. I began to feel relaxed, then I noticed a buzzing in the back of my head. That soon turned to pulsing and I could feel the area around my neck really heat up. Next there was a sensation of letting go… and the headache was gone.."

"This is my favorite exercise. I lie on my back in my "Reiki Room," and find myself feeling comfortable in being me. My inner vision improves and it's easier to see the big picture."

journal

Theme Four: Crown
Right hand on the crown of head, left hand circles neck at base of skull.

Statement of Intent: (*Example*) It is my intention to get in touch with my inner wisdom.

Method: (*Example*) Mentally connecting with all those who wish for the best for mankind, place your hands as directed above. Trust that your cosmic, highest self will assist in experiencing vigor in your efforts. Become mindful of expanding in a system of limitless potential. Focus upon potential within that system. Know yourself in an energetic sense. You are in process... Now, allow yourself to honor and to accept the 'brilliance" about You!

Your Statement of Intent:

Your Method: (as above, or...)

Recipient's Impressions

"This exercise that boosts my sense of spaciousness, as an idea creating, energizing tonic to my creativity."

"An individual who was very upset because he'd just be outplaced, visibly relaxed during this theme. As the therapist, I noticed the softening and change in his face. Later I asked him about it. He told me that it was when I got to this position that he remembered: "answers come long after they're expected..." That bit of inner wisdom reminded him that the job loss was understandable, if not right now, then sometime down the road."

journal

Theme Five: Throat
Hands float over throat area, one set of fingers atop the other, just beneath chin, and above collar bones. Thumbs in.

Statement of Intent: (*Example*) It is my intent to boost my capacity to communicate clearly (throat) and to lessen the tension that arises from misunderstandings.

Method: (*Example*) Draw energy to the intention to become eloquent. You *know* the ability to communicate fluently. Conversations are now lively. You speak with conviction.

Your Statement of Intent:

Your Method: (as above, or...)

Recipient's Impressions

"I called my old friend, Ann today to ask her if she'd feel comfortable doing a Reiki session even though my throat was very sore and I had a temperature. She gave me the green light so we met. She asked me how things were going for me with my new boss. Was everything else, except my throat, O.K.?

I shut down. I didn't want to talk about the changes going on at work, and how sales quotas and commissions were messing with my peace of mind, so she started, but when her hands were above my throat, I began to clear my throat repeatedly and to swallow over and over, real hard. And then the pain turned fuzzy.

Afterwards, we talked about how I felt (much better). The physical improvement was not all that happened. I could also tell my friend how stressful things were at work.

journal

Relax, Open, Celebrate! A 21-Day Program for Reiki and Relaxation

9

Unbroken Wholeness

Coming out of Elsewhere,
as we do -
To fogs and bogs
and city blues,
Stepping into Somewhere,
as we do -
Into a place, and into Time,
Some think we're but fragments, far
and few -
Shards, with a prismatic view,
By heaven's winds blown all askew,
Dismembered bits, of different hues,
And risk, in all that ballyhoo,
A sense of Life, Divine.

Wind-in-the-Feather

Buddha was once asked, "Are you a god?"
He replied, "No."
"Are you an angel then?"
He said, "No."
"Well, then, what are you?"
"I am awake," he said.

The 21-Day Program for
Reiki and Relaxation

The Usui System of Reiki has proven to be an avenue for many to alleviate tension, manage stress and expand powers of perception. Reiki amplifies and accelerates awareness of Self in dynamic relationship to the Whole. Thus, tuning-in to Self and its underlying, complex patterns is simplified with the practice of Reiki.

When practiced as a renewal of commitment to self-care, of sponsoring the elimination of toxic substances and emotions, the Reiki practice becomes an ongoing, reconnecting device, always available, even in busiest moments. Reiki practice is an opportunity to tap-in to your own highest wisdom. You can become adept at listening to body messages. Paying attention to intuitive feelings, and responding to them, is facilitated. The possibilities are limitless when fostered by the harmonious, coherent state which the practice of Reiki evokes. Over the years, I have come *to see things in new ways*. And so can you.

One effective way to devleop a sense of the harmonious-coherent state is to practice Reiki in a dedicated 21 - Day Program (modeled on the example of Dr. Mikao Usui). This sets the stage for integrating the creative, life-affirming process into your daily routine. The program has only two working parts. One: Before the Reiki Session, focus your intent. Two: Be consistent in the practice and keep track of what is going on in your practice by jotting down memos/notes soon asfter the session.

A good way to explore Reiki is through a program designed to encourage relaxation. When you are relaxed, it is easier to connect with your best self and boundless possibilities. So, go ahead and try out the program on the following pages at your own convenience.

You may wish to begin *The 21 - Day Reiki and Relaxation Program* after you have completed *Reiki* I Training, or practitioners have done The 21 - Day Program both before and after their training, and say each is effective. *After* the training, the creative opportunities within the 21-Day regime are more apparent and experienced *in new ways*. You already have all the tools you need to attain a "harmonious - coherent" state, so let your own inner wisdom be your guide as to the timing.

We now turn our attention to the following focal points. These can serve as springboards to focus the process as you begin your ***21-Day Reiki and Relaxation Program:***

Focal Points

Springboard group discussion, or review in quiet, personal moments the items that follow.

1. **Focal Point: Wisdom of Elders**
   What would the great awakened geniuses of the world have to say about my/our relationship with the practice of Reiki and its place in the global community?

2. **Focal Point: Visualization**
   What would it be like to go about my/our life in resonance with compassionate "energy medicine"?

3. **Focal Point: Self-Inventory**
   What is needed for me/us to remember how I/we "process" - in the practice of Reiki, a "being" artform?

4. **Focal Point: Awareness**
   What's the way to best express Reiki given my process and a member of both physical and energetic realms?

5. **Focal Point: Sensory Awareness**
   What is my physicality telling me and how does that dovetail with my energetic experience?

6. **Focal Point: Harmonious - Coherent States**
   When am I most likely to be in harmony with my inner truth - my best self? And how does this relate to the practice of Reiki?

7. **Focal Point: Empathy**
   When am I most in harmony with others and how does this relate to the practice of Reiki - and then to the living global community?

How to Use the 21-Day
Reiki and Relaxation
Program

The 21-Day program can be used by both the uninitiated and the experienced Reiki practitioner. If you have not completed Reiki I Training, simply pick one area of the body, or one issue that concerns you to concentrate upon each day.

If you have completed Reiki I Training you will do well to focus on a different hand position each day.

If you are a Second Degree Student, or have completed this level, remember to incorporate the specific things you learned in that Training.

These charts and outlines require your commitment to take good care of You. They will be effective only if *You* make them so.

Just for today, Relax into the homeplace of celebrating pure potential.

Example:
Focusing Intent

Day One: Eyes
**Hands just above strained, tired, irritated eyes, fingers
toegther - relaxed setting - eyes closed.**

Statement of Intent: It is my intent to release tension
around my eyes, and to see things "in new way."

Mind: accelerated creative "vision"

Body: relaxed eye muscles

Emotions: "seeing" different viewpoints

Inner-Spirit: visionary spirit for new global
perspective

Special Challenge: release of out-moded viewpoints/
biases

Method Memo: Draw energy to the intent to view
physical and mental challenges from
a new perspective. Release visual barriers.
See with twinkling eyes.

Your 21 - Day Reiki and Relaxation Program
Focusing Intent:

Day One: _____

Statement of Intent:

Mind:

Body:

Emotions:

Inner-Spirit:

Special Challenge:

Method Memo:

journal

Your 21 - Day Reiki and Relaxation Program
Focusing Intent:

Day Two: _____

Statement of Intent:

Mind:

Body:

Emotions:

Inner-Spirit:

Special Challenge:

Method Memo:

journal

Your 21 - Day Reiki and Relaxation Program
Focusing Intent:

Day Three: _____

Statement of Intent:

Mind:

Body:

Emotions:

Inner-Spirit:

Special Challenge:

journal

Your 21 - Day Reiki and Relaxation Program
Focusing Intent:

Day Four: _____

Statement of Intent:

Mind:

Body:

Emotions:

Inner-Spirit:

Special Challenge:

Method Memo:

journal

Your 21 - Day Reiki and Relaxation Program
Focusing Intent:

Day Five: _____

Statement of Intent:

Mind:

Body:

Emotions:

Inner-Spirit:

Special Challenge:

Method Memo:

journal

Your 21 - Day Reiki and Relaxation Program
Focusing Intent:

Day Six: _____

Statement of Intent:

Mind:

Body:

Emotions:

Inner-Spirit:

Special Challenge:

Method Memo:

journal

Your 21 - Day Reiki and Relaxation Program
Focusing Intent:

Day Seven: _____

Statement of Intent:

Mind:

Body:

Emotions:

Inner-Spirit:

Special Challenge:

Method Memo:

journal

Release Tension

Date: _____

Fill in the columns below. Observe tension release. Record for later review

Mind	Body	Emotions	Inner-Spirit
10	10	10	10
9	9	9	9
8	8	8	8
7	7	7	7
6	6	6	6
5	5	5	5
4	4	4	4
3	3	3	3
2	2	2	2
1	1	1	1

10 = High Tension
1 = Low Tension

21 - Day Reiki and Relaxation Program
Tracking Chart (Days 1-7)

Track feelings and responses by
using this chart .
Check the day and hour, and note
your response to this
stress dissolving regime.

	Sun	Mon	Tues	Wed	Thurs	Fri	Sat
Hour							
1							
2							
3							
4							
5							
6							
7							
8							
9							
10							
11							
12							

Day/ Date

Your 21 - Day Reiki and Relaxation Program
Focusing Intent:

Day Eight: _____

Statement of Intent:

Mind:

Body:

Emotions:

Inner-Spirit:

Special Challenge:

Method Memo:

journal

Your 21 - Day Reiki and Relaxation Program
Focusing Intent:

***

Day Nine: _____

Statement of Intent:

Mind:

Body:

Emotions:

Inner-Spirit:

Special Challenge:

Method Memo:

journal

Your 21 - Day Reiki and Relaxation Program
Focusing Intent:

Day Ten: _____

Statement of Intent:

Mind:

Body:

Emotions:

Inner-Spirit:

Special Challenge:

Method Memo:

journal

Your 21 - Day Reiki and Relaxation Program
Focusing Intent:

<hr>

Day Eleven: _____

Statement of Intent:

Mind:

Body:

Emotions:

Inner-Spirit:

Special Challenge:

Method Memo:

journal

Your 21 - Day Reiki and Relaxation Program
Focusing Intent:

Day Twelve: _____

Statement of Intent:

Mind:

Body:

Emotions:

Inner-Spirit:

Special Challenge:

Method Memo:

journal

Your 21 - Day Reiki and Relaxation Program
Focusing Intent:

Day Thirteen: _____

Statement of Intent:

Mind:

Body:

Emotions:

Inner-Spirit:

Special Challenge:

Method Memo:

journal

Your 21 - Day Reiki and Relaxation Program
Focusing Intent:

Day Fourteen: _____

Statement of Intent:

Mind:

Body:

Emotions:

Inner-Spirit:

Special Challenge:

Method Memo:

journal

Release Tension

Date: _____

Fill in the columns below.
Observe tension release.
Record for later review

10	10	10	10
9	9	9	9
8	8	8	8
7	7	7	7
6	6	6	6
5	5	5	5
4	4	4	4
3	3	3	3
2	2	2	2
1	1	1	1
Mind	Body	Emotions	Inner-Spirit

10 = High Tension
1 = Low Tension

21 - Day Reiki and Relaxation Program
Tracking Chart (Days 8-14)

Track feelings and responses by using this chart .
Check the day and hour, and note your response to this stress dissolving regime.

	Sun	Mon	Tues	Wed	Thurs	Fri	Sat
				Day/ Date			
Hour							
1							
2							
3							
4							
5							
6							
7							
8							
9							
10							
11							
12							

Your 21 - Day Reiki and Relaxation Program
Focusing Intent:

Day Fifteen: _____

Statement of Intent:

Mind:

Body:

Emotions:

Inner-Spirit:

Special Challenge:

Method Memo:

journal

Your 21 - Day Reiki and Relaxation Program
Focusing Intent:

Day Sixteen: _____

Statement of Intent:

Mind:

Body:

Emotions:

Inner-Spirit:

Special Challenge:

Method Memo:

journal

Your 21 - Day Reiki and Relaxation Program
Focusing Intent:

Day Seventeen: _____

Statement of Intent:

Mind:

Body:

Emotions:

Inner-Spirit:

Special Challenge:

Method Memo:

journal

Your 21 - Day Reiki and Relaxation Program
Focusing Intent:

Day Eighteen: _____

Statement of Intent:

Mind:

Body:

Emotions:

Inner-Spirit:

Special Challenge:

Method Memo:

journal

"Quantum physics, long to be grasped, has shown us a new universe. A wholistic, observer - participant universe that has the potential for 'hidden variables'… this hiddenous is an alluding towards a cosmic inwardness (in which we begin) to grasp our planet and cosmos as a total system.."

Beatrix Murrell

Your 21 - Day Reiki and Relaxation Program
Focusing Intent:

Day Nineteen: _____

Statement of Intent:

Mind:

Body:

Emotions:

Inner-Spirit:

Special Challenge:

Method Memo:

journal

Your 21 - Day Reiki and Relaxation Program
Focusing Intent:

Day Twenty: _____

Statement of Intent:

Mind:

Body:

Emotions:

Inner-Spirit:

Special Challenge:

Method Memo:

journal

"Show Gratitude..."

Mikao Usui

Your 21 - Day Reiki and Relaxation Program
Focusing Intent:

Day Twenty-One: _____

Statement of Intent:

Mind:

Body:

Emotions:

Inner-Spirit:

Special Challenge:

Method Memo:

journal

ReleaseTension

Date: _____

Fill in the columns below.
Observe tension release.
Record for later review

Mind	Body	Emotions	Inner-Spirit
10	10	10	10
9	9	9	9
8	8	8	8
7	7	7	7
6	6	6	6
5	5	5	5
4	4	4	4
3	3	3	3
2	2	2	2
1	1	1	1

10 = High Tension
1 = Low Tension

21 - Day Reiki and Relaxation Program
Tracking Chart (Days 9-21)

Track feelings and responses by using this chart .
Check the day and hour, and note your response to this stress dissolving regime.

Hour	Sun	Mon	Tues	Wed	Thurs	Fri	Sat
Day/ Date							
1							
2							
3							
4							
5							
6							
7							
8							
9							
10							
11							
12							

three bows and ten thousand well wishes

Summary

The 21-Day Reiki and Relaxation Program takes us within, to become students of ourselves. As you review your Charts, Focusing Intent, and Journaling Commentaries, it is likely that you will notice that a change has occurred. You have communicated with yourself... body, mind, and inner-spirit in an attentive and appreciative way. You have honored your Being, and your Beingness.

Whether you allotted 10 or 15 mintues, once or twice a day, or spent more time and then communed with Nature matters not - if you learned what you needed to know and found that for which you searched. The coherent, harmonious state is at hand, and you have touched it!

This program is always available to you. If it is your wish, please incorporate it into your daily routine or return to it at intervals. Having completed it, you must now ask yourself, as Usui did, WHAT'S NEXT?!

Congratulations, and may Life, as it has a way of doing, provide all that You need!

"Crafted by our own hands, we create a uniquely expressed life that isthe calling from within."

Phyllis Lei Furumoto
In a letter to the worldwide community of Reiki Masters

APPENDIX A: MAKING CONTACT

A.   *Takata*

One December day, in 1980, Hawayo Takata made her transition leaving behind a legacy, many students, and twenty-two teachers of Reiki, (*The Usui System of Natural Healing)*. She had spent almost four decades sharing her wisdom. Her students had learned to treat Reiki with the respect it deserves. Her interest (as had been that of her teacher, Hayashi, and his teacher, Usui) was in helping people to awaken to their own sacred place in the universe. With this realization, she taught, comes healing - on many levels.

Hawayo Takata was born on Christmas Eve in Kauai, Hawaii where she grew up, was married, widowed at an early age and where she called home. She found Reiki in the way so many of its practitioners have - by fortuitous detours and happy twists of fate. (Her story has been told in depth by Fran Brown, in <u>Living Reiki, Takata's Teachings</u>).

"With Reiki there is always hope."

Hawayo Takata

B.   Organizations

Reiki Masters of *The Usui System of Reiki* may be contacted through the Reiki Alliance, which was formed by the original 22 Reiki Masters trained by Takata to lend support to its members and to maintain the integrity of *The Usui System of Reiki*. Masters of the Reiki Alliance follow definite professional standards set forth in a Statement of Identity, and teach in the format taught by Takata.

1.   **The Reiki Alliance**
P. O. Box 41
Cataldo, ID 83810, USA
Phone: 1/208/682-3535
Fax: 1/208/682-4848
E-mail: 74051.3471@compuserve.com

2.   **Reiki Outreach International**
P. O. Box 609
Fairoaks, California 95628
916/863-1500
Fax 916/863-6464

3.   **International Association of Reiki**
Lesni 14
46001 Liberec 1
Czech Republic

4.   **http://www.onedegreebeyond.com/reiki**
for more organizations

C.   *L*ocating a Reiki Master

The Initial Interview

1.   Tell me a little bit about yourself, and your background, and how you became a Reiki Master.

2.   Tell me a little bit about *The Usui System of Reiki.*

3.   How long have you been involved in Reiki? Did it take you a long time to become a Reiki Master? What is your lineage?

4.   I've heard that Reiki can be effective in stress management. Is that true? Are there any other ways that Reiki can help me?

5.   How do you view your role in a Reiki Session?

6.   Do you aim Reiki? Or how do you "get" it?

7.   Who *does* the Reiki?

8.   How did you come to teach Reiki? Are you a member of an organization? re you certified to do hands-on work?

9.   Do you have any long term students?

10.   When can you speak to yourself from the center of the universe?

> *"The continuation of life on this planet in a healthy way and within a healthy environment requires our attitudes encompass all possibilities and that we monitor ourselves responsibly, while continuing to offer ourselves and our gifts to all."*
>
> *Earlene F. Gleisner, R.N.*
> <u>*Reiki in Everyday Living*</u>

*Q*uestions to Ask Yourself

1. Does this person seem sincere and dedicated?

2. Was this person willing to spend at least half an hour talking and sharing with me?

3. Did this person say "I" often, and in a controlling way, and answer from Ego?

4. Did this person seem mature?

5. Was there a definite spark of enthusiasm when Usui was discussed? What kind of depth and bond to *The Usui System* did you notice?

6. Did this Reiki Master display mastery by being able to answer the question "When can you speak to your self, from the center of the Universe?"

7. Did you like this person?

8. Does this person seem to be someone you could respect?

9. Would *you* want to know this person over a long period of time?

10. What did *you* learn from your conversation?

*M*aking Contact

Reiki is fast becoming popular as its promise for well-being is recognized. There are Reiki "gatherings," "drop-ins," "circles," popping up like spring flowers in most large cities and even in the most remote villages. Some of these gatherings are on-going support groups for initiated practitioners. Some are meetings in which the Reiki *experience* is available to those interested in a "test drive." Most Reiki Masters of *The Usui System of Reiki* (those who can trace their lineage directly to him), offer an introductory evening in which a brief Reiki *experience* is also a possibility.

*L*ocating a Gathering

1.   Contact the Reiki Alliance for the phone number of
       a Reiki Master near you.

       The Reiki Alliance
       P. O. Box 41
       Cataldo, ID 83810, **USA**
       Phone: 1/208/682-3535
       Fax: 1/208/682-4848
       E-mail: 74051.3471@compuserve.com

       Stichting the Reiki Alliance - Europe
       Postlous 75523 1070 AM
       Amsterdam NETHERLANDS
       Phone: 31-20-6719276
       Fax: 31-20-6711736
       E-mail: 100125.466@compuserve.com

2.   Check your local phone book, newspaper, bulletin boards...do
       some leg work and personal investigation including interviewing
       the Reiki Master involved.

APPENDIX B: COMPLEMENTARY SYSTEMS

A.   *C*onscious Breathing

1.   Lie down on your back. Make sure you are comfortable, and on a comfortable surface.

2.   Your legs should be stretched out…your feet about a foot apart.

3.   Let your arms rest at your sides.

4.   Breathe very slowly, and become *aware* of your breathing.

5.   Visualize, as you inhale, a scale filling with soft mountain air, refreshing you, then tipping, *slowly* releasing, in a *slow* out-breath, releasing tension and… as you let go of each breath...

6.   Take long, *slow*, breaths... in and out... all the way to the last of each... pause after you exhale— WAIT until your body nudges you to inhale.

7.   When that happens, **consciously** take a long, peaceful, *slow*, breath - in.

      (This process may take a few seconds or fifteen or thirty seconds…)

8. **Don't hold your breath, but just let it gently slide into the next in/out - as you visualize the scale balancing, moving slowly in rhythm with your breathing.**

9. Allow your eyes to close as you focus on your breathing, now very deep and regular... balancing back and forth from way down to way up as you continue visualizing the scale.

10. Breathe in through your nose. *Slowly.*

11. Breathe out through your mouth. *Gently.*

12. RELAX your body and let all the aches, pains, pressures float away with each exhale.

13. Each breath you inhale brings with it peace and comfort as you breathe in the restful energy that is about you.

B.   *R*eiki and Therapeutic Touch

You may be familiar with the work of Dolores Krieger, Ph.D., RN., and her colleague, Dora Kunz. In the very early 1970's, they developed a technique called Therapeutic Touch. This technique is widely practiced within the established medical community and is similar to Reiki, *The Usui System of Natural Healing* (also widely practiced there) in a number of ways.

Both Reiki and Therapeutic Touch operate on the premise that *imbalance* in the human energy field (HEF,) detectable by changes in patterns of energy, can disrupt the natural state, which is Wellness. Both these modalities also posit that in supporting a modulation of the field, we are simply actualizing that potential for Wellness. However, the manner in which the Reiki methodology views the exchange in relation to Universal Life Force differs from that of Therapeutic Touch.

In *The Usui System of Reiki*, energy is *drawn*, not *directed*. Whereas those practicing Therapeutic Touch attempt to "aim" energy. Although both Therapeutic Touch and Reiki assume empathic intentionality and ask for committed "centeredness", *ego-less* transmission of energy is central to *The Usui System*. In Reiki, although we try to be ever mindful of, and sensitive to, the HEF, we recognize our limitations in interpreting the emanations from that field and are not attached to making assessments. In the treatment of others, where Therapeutic Touch proceeds from the centering process, to *evaluate* the HEF, Reiki simply *pays attention*.

Although in both practices we need not actually make physical contact, the Reiki touch *is* just that; a non-invasive, focused, light tactile interaction with our own or another's subtle energy field.

Finally, from the perspective of the Collective Consciousness, both methodologies conjoin in the desire for Wellness as a Worldview.

APPENDIX C: RESOURCES

A. Suggested Reading

Achterberg, Jeanne, *Imagery in Healing*, New Seneca Library, Boston, Mass., 1985.

Barber, Ph.D, Theodore Xenophon, *The Human Nature of Birds*, St. Martins Press, New York, NY, 1993.

Barnett, Libby and Chambers, Maggie, *Reiki, Energy Medicine*, Healing Arts Press, Rochester, VT, 1996.

Benson, Herbert, M.D., *The Relaxation Response*, Berkley Press, New York, NY, 1987.

Bohm, David, *Unfolding Meaning,* ARK Paperbacks, Rutledge, London, 1994.

Bohm, David, *Wholeness & the Implicate Order,* Rutledge, London, 1983.

Bohm, David and Hiley, Basil J., *The Undivided Universe,* Rutledge, London, 1994.

Cohen, Michael J., *Reconnecting with Nature*, Ecopress, Corvallis, OR, 1997.

Davies, Paul, *The Cosmic Blueprint*, Simon & Schuster, New York, NY, 1988.

Dossey, Larry, M.D., *Space, Time and Medicine*, Shambala Publications, Inc., Boston, Mass., 1982.

Ford, Clyde, *Where Healing Waters Meet*, Station Hill Press, Barrytown, NY, 1989.

Fox, Matthew, *The Reinvention of Work*, Harper-Collins, New York, NY, 1994.

Fox, Matthew and Rupert Sheldrake, *Natural Grace*, Doubleday Publishers, New York, NY, 1996.

Fox, Matthew and Rupert Sheldrake, *The Physics of Angels*, Harper-Collins Publishers, New York, NY, 1996.

Fox, Matthew, *Original Blessing*, Bear & Co., Santa Fe, NM, 1983.

Gerber, Richard, M.D., *Vibrational Medicine*, Bear & Company, Inc., Santa Fe, NM, 1988.

Gleisner, R.N., Earlene F., *Reiki in Everyday Living*, White Feather Press, Laytonville, CA, 1992.

Griffin, David Ray, *The Reenchantment of Science*, Postmodern Proposals, State University of New York Press, Albany, NY, 1988.

Grof, Stanislav, *Beyond the Brain*, State University of New York Press, Albany, NY, 1985.

Grof, Stanislav, *The Adventures of Self Discovery*, State University of New York Press, Albany, NY, 1985.

Hall, Mari, *Practical Reiki*, Thorsons, London, 1997.

Hendricks, Gay, Ph.D., *Conscious Breathing*, Bantam Books, New York, NY, 1995.

Horan, Paula, Ph.D., *Abundance Through Reiki*, Lotus Light Publications, Harper San Francisco, New York, NY, 1992.

Horan, Paula, Ph.D., *Empowerment Through Reiki*, Lotus Light Publications, Wilmot, WI, 1989.

Krishnamurti, J. and Bohm, David, *The Ending of Time*, Harper-Collins, San Francisco, CA 1985.

Mackenzie, Donald A., *Myths of Japan*, Gramercy Books, New York, NY, 1994.

Mitchell, Paul David, *The Usui System of Natural Healing*, Couer d' Alene, ID, 1985.

Myss, Caroline, *Anatomy of the Spirit*, Crown Publishers, New York, NY, 1996.

Pribam, Karl, *Languages of the Brain*, Wadsworth Publishing, Monterey, CA, 1977.

Russell, Peter, *The White Hole in Time*, Harper San Francisco, New York, NY, 1992.

Shealy, Norman, M.D., Ph.D., and Myss, Caroline, *The Creation of Health*, Stillpoint Publishing, Walpole, NH, 1993.

Sheldrake, Rupert, *A New Science of Life,* Blond & Briggs, London, 1981.

Swimme, Brian, *The Universe is a Green Dragon*, Bear and Company, Inc., Santa Fe, NM, 1985.

Swimme, Brian, *The Hidden Heart of the Cosmos*, Orbis Books, New York, NY, 1996

Swimme, Brian and Berry, Thomas, *The Universe Story*, Harper-Collins Publishers, New York, NY, 1992.

Talbot, Michael, *The Holographic Universe*, Harper Collins, New York, NY, 1991.

Teilhard de Chardin, Pierre, *The Future of Man*, Harper & Row, New York, NY, 1959.

Twan, Wanja, In the Light of a Distant Star, Morning Star Productions, Vancouver, B.C., Canada

Weil, Andrew, M.D., *Spontaneous Healing*, Alfred A. Snopf, Inc., New York, NY, 1995.

Wilber, Ken, *A Brief History of Everything*, Shambhala, Boston, 1996.

Weiss, Brian L., M.D., *Through Time into Healing*, Fireside Book, Simon & Shuster, New York, NY, 1992.

B.   Suggested "Surfing"

<u>One Degree Beyond… (*and its links*)</u>
http://www.onedegreebeyond.com
http://www.onedegreebeyond.com/reiki

<u>Project NatureConnect</u>
Institute of Global Education
http://www.pacificrim.net/nature/.www.html

<u>Union of Concerned Scientists</u>
http://www.vcsvsa.org/warning.html

<u>New and Alternative Theories of Physics</u>
http://www.weburbia.com/pg/theories.htm
http://www.weburbia.demon.co.uk/pg/theories.htm

APPENDIX D: A QUIZ

Integrating Reiki into Your Daily Life
Smiling at Earth Mother

	Often	*Sometimes*	*No*
1. Do I take time to relax and reflect upon my spiritual path?	❐	❐	❐
2. Do I spend time experiencing Nature and it wonders?	❐	❐	❐
3. Do I encourage others towards change and innovation?	❐	❐	❐
4. Do I value cooperation over competition?	❐	❐	❐
5. Is Reiki something I practice with an understanding of its place from a whole systems perspective?	❐	❐	❐
6. Do I value and honor diversity?	❐	❐	❐
7. Do I see the interrelated and interdependent nature of Earth and Earthlings?	❐	❐	❐
8. Do I value the process of differentiation?	❐	❐	❐
9. Do I ascribe to the metaphor of "tapestry" as opposed to "melting pot"?	❐	❐	❐
10. Have I learned the process of dialogue as opposed to aggression/confrontation?	❐	❐	❐

	Often	*Sometimes*	*No*
11. How familiar am I with dialogue, visualization, team learning?	❐	❐	❐
12. Am I coming to see the value of lifestyle choices which are simpler, less consumer-oriented?	❐	❐	❐
13. Am I connecting with others who are also keeping a "good-eye" on the processof positive change?	❐	❐	❐
14. Do I <u>trust</u> on the unfolding dance of order?	❐	❐	❐
Am I ready to move beyond a mechanistic, consumer-oriented worldview?	❐	❐	❐
16. Am I coming to see the universe as a dynamic, interconnected whole, within which I contribute as a harmonious participant?	❐	❐	❐

If you scored over 8 in the first two columns, you are beginning to keep a focused eye on the global community.

If you scored less than 8, we are pleased to know that you are here, learning about these new perspectives.

Appendices   277

INDEX

About the Author

Janeanne Narrin, M.A., C.S.W., whose background is in Industrial Psychology and Business (her career spans many years in management consulting) is a master teacher in *The Usui System of Reiki.* Her interest in the effects of stress on personnel in the workplace prompted her to actively seek out innovative stress release techniques. While on this search, she discovered Reiki, a methodology she describes as wedding contemporary scientific knowledge with age-old insight.

"It's a system that encourages its practitioners to empower themselves," she says. "Reiki's something you access to relieve and dissolve stress. It also has tremendous restorative potential," she concludes.

When her schedule doesn't find her on the seminar trail, Ms. Narrin continues to pursue her interests in writing, painting, poetry and photography.

To receive information about current workshops offered, please contact her at the following address:

P. O. Box 2324
Friday Harbor, WA 98250

*L*ET US KNOW WHAT YOU THINK

We at *Little White Buffalo Publishing Cottage* honor the tradition of indigenous peoples throughout the world who share their insights and wisdom through collaboration and storytelling. Our icon, the Little White Buffalo, symbol of communion for "all of our relations" expresses our wholehearted wish to explore, illuminate, support, and nurture common bonds, as we, a global community, move beyond our own limits to seek our full potential in harmony with Natural Law.

We invite your participation and comments. To receive current information about other titles, please contact us at this address:

Little White Buffalo Publishing Cottage
12345 Lake City Way, N.E., Suite 204
Seattle, Washington 98125
Phone or Fax: 425/673-9325